THROUGH THE CENTRE

TO THE RIVER

"Don't forget to look out of the window and remember the colours you see!"

Helen Sharman – Astronaut

© 2017 All work copyright of the author

Front cover artwork: Journey To The Centre by Nicola Troll

Back cover design by Paul Helm

A CIP record for this book is available from the British Library.

This edition published by **SennenDawn** 2017

SennenDawn / London SW19

sennendawn@gmail.com

ISBN 978-0-9935299-1-7

This book could not have happened without the help of all those people who spoke with me as I walked the paths around London. Strangers I met once or maybe twice who shared their own stories: thank you.

Also, for constant support, thanks to:

Margaret & John Cluett, Charlotte Martin, Paul Nathan, Abi Palmer, Lucy Allen, Liz Warren, Nicola Troll, Keith, Jackie, Alex & Hannah Pengelley, Joe Duggan, Tahira Haq, Jackie Maye, Sharon Lukosius, Karen Hunt, John Bishop, Catherine Jane Howard Schiff, Melissa Goring, Mary Wadia, Janet Ivins Orr, Sue Turbett, Marjan Bartlett-Freriks, Neil Gillespie, Dave Wallis and Helen's high school classmates: Helen Addis, Joyce Gillespie, and Fran Wallis.

In memory of my mother-in-law, Connie Bishop, whose voice echoes in these pages and of our friend Lizzie Thomas.

For James

who walks and talks me
through

A Note about the author

TIM SLADER is the author of *Ways to Bottle Sunshine*

Because of Kathmandu his whole life changed so much for the better.

THROUGH THE CENTRE
TO THE RIVER

Tim Slader

Chapter

IF YOU HAVE A
PREFERRED ROUTE
PLEASE NOTIFY THE
DRIVER AT THE START OF
THE JOURNEY

Through The Centre to the River

"It isn't far to walk."
"I think it isn't too far to walk."

<u>i</u>

Ended up on a housing estate
Or just that kind of place I suppose
Some such home as steel fortress.
Private: residents only.
No Cold Calling Area.
No Uninvited Sales Persons.
After half an hour
Knocking on all sorts of doors
It turns out he wasn't there.
He really was sick.
He was actually back where I'd started.
He grabbed me,
Half-filled the white enamel mugs,
Those with a chipped blue ribbon on the lip,
And began
Talking in toasts.

Say no more,
I played that role.
Say no more,
I played that role for him.
He deserved it.
In the Catholic faith,

He deserved it.
A memory of jungle,
It's half way between
And she had a boyfriend.
He's English.
He left then turned up
So they knew about me
Happily moving positions,
Faces and shapes around.

What date is it?
28th. Why?
Are you supposed to be
Somewhere else?

South-facing windows,
Perfect just like the Hill
As sun sets.
It's time.
Let's go,
So I turned to Colliers Wood.

Raspberry juice,
As dark as blood,
Fills the pavement cracks.
Someone blows the whistle
And FOLLER, ELP, LUCKSNAP,
SLANG-LABRAT, BOLX,
LAMZ, JOSHIE, PIEZ,
Each & every one
A king or queen
In this shifting-sand castle,
(note LUV U GUYS 4 EV
Keep safe.)
Riding paper aeroplanes,
Glance down from the walkway.

In the early hours,
Captain Bee staggers home, drunk
On nectar and shorts.
A he or she?
Impossible to see
Beneath the thick bumble
Layers of the fancy dress costume.
Modern day some little Puck
At a quarter to three
And desperate for a wee
Caught short against a tree
So many layers, struggles to get free.
Now at least we know for certain
That dear, virtuous Captain Bee's a he.
Righting wrongs, humming humble songs,
Long days since his starring role
In the school's twice Christmas assembly.

Phone's hanging off the hook,
Slot clogged with chewing gum.
Everything round here
Is going up for sale.
Like Linda's.
I shouldn't think
Anyone would be mad enough
To buy that maisonette
With water running down the walls,
Stink bugs clinging
To the spray-textured ceilings.
Find it safer than the disappearing trees.
Two up, two down.
Went up the stairs.
No bedroom doors,
Smoked over glass.
Her father used one room

As a bottle and apple store
And for a time it suited her.
Then she got those yap-rats.
Don't tread on the yip-rats.
I can't think ever why.
Must be all round her legs,
In the doors.
I suppose,
They're something to fall over.
Or perhaps they're well trained
To keep away from strange feet.
The sun doesn't get round
At the window here
Until dinner time
And, I suppose, there was never much
To do tomorrow.
Her mother,
Who gossips said was over
Swan Lane Park
In the sandpits
With the young beaus,
Well, she got gout.
Got to keep her feet up.

I've got to keep my feet up.
Thought it was safer
On those bloody water tablets.
It was supposed to rain anyway.
So it settled things nicely.
Still, I don't know where we are going
Or rather where we were going.
And you all dressed up Henry,
Which wife are you out with today?
Gilly from the kitchen?
Lauren Amy from the nursery?
Sarah from the swimming pool?

Louise from the magician's assistants?
Faye from the clinic?
Bibi from the Polish plumbers?

So talking about Linda
As you do.
Things aren't very good
With her and Vinnie.
Asked him how he was
He stayed the silent type
That doesn't suit her:
"As I have to be the subject
Of all the conversation."
Nice hotel weekend,
I think she said they went to bed,
Went along the beach certainly.
She wasn't too excited.
He's supposed to be coming tomorrow -
Ice cream party.
Don't think there's going to be
Too many strawberries, do you?
A fellow won't sit down under that.
Although, being a Scotsman, he might.
He hasn't met the woof-rats, I suppose.
Love in dribs and drabs.

Not a bit like your daughter
And her young man.
Close as clams.
Went to Deal, didn't they?
Went to Rye, didn't they?
Went to Morecombe, didn't they?
Went to Sennen, didn't they?
Do you think
They'll ever get married?
You look at him

Looking at her
And you see he's smitten for her
And she's smitten for him.
Besotted is a word to use.
Who would have thought it?
Getting close in the Far East
And closer still on the Indian Subcontinent.

And all the while that Linda with
Just the bed upstairs.
Don't know if she has a cupboard.
Up for sale though.
Don't know how much they want for it,
I haven't been by for a time.
She likes old buildings.
Her front door is going to be up those steps.
I couldn't go up them in these heels.
She said come in round the back.
I don't know how many people she'll have
Offering.

Here they are:
Not so bad after all people,
Bright-side people.

The caretaker,
For what it's worth,
Rests on his pink cushion
Swivel-chair, round and round,
And scans the row of CCTV monitors.
Feels he controls everything;
The king of the concrete empire.
Watches the knee-tremblers
In the furthest corners.
But in all sincerity
These random sparks hold momentary interest

As do the burning-out cars,
Vocal broken relationships,
And vague vanishings into thin air
Inside doors and out.
Let us take a moment to look deeper,
Beyond the Sunday songs
Lamenting the Old Country,
Beyond our Mother's ruin,
Beyond the constant rattling of a dog's chain
And the fact that there's just enough light.
Into
A cloistered domain of
Rough breeze-block walls,
Ill-set grouting,
The sizzled electric smell
Of shrink wrapped wiring
And the water pulsing
Through silver foil lagged pipes.
The scent of a cramped changing-room
Closed to the public.
A blend of disinfectant and stolen sweat.
With a tot of Christmas whisky
The security of four walls
And the company of concrete gnomes.
Yet in his dreams:
Come on you Spurs.
Listen, I'll tell anyone:
Alan John Gilzean is a god.
King of The Lane.
Him and Greavsie.
Him and Chivers.
Dad used to bump into him
Round Chingford back in the day.
Private man. Legend.
Happy Days.
As Big Mouth Billy Bass

Twists, tail twitching, sings:
Don't worry. Be happy.

Lacy curtains twitch and grind.
Friendly to your face,
A tinkeress behind your back
Sharpening the final blade:
A toothless dam
Worrying a chicken's bone.
Pumped up importance
In a bunch of keys.
And if looks could kill...
Well, she'd be so sorry
To hear what happened to you.

Katrina, a Monday to Friday
Quiet young lady,
Name in pink chalk
Across the paving stones,
Fancied cheese on toast.
Put it in the toaster
Sideways on.
Bang!
Daft as a brush.
Why do people say that?

Now the cowboy is putting in the posts.
Soon the walls will be skinned
To reveal pink shower curtains
And white leather sofas
Walls almost naked.
Count the satellite dishes.
Read the messages:
Suck your mum.
Tasha Cohen is butters!
The tarmac covered with white explosions,

Paint cans tipped three floors down
End over end.
Here are the piles of wooden doors,
Here are the burnt duvets,
Here are the crisped flowers,
The wreaths and the crosses.
War zone crumpled Carling cans,
Fray Bentos Just Chicken pies
And
No fly tipping.
So I saw them
Pouring bitumen down the stairs.
I've got a list of names.
I know who pushed the brick walls over.
Pigeons flap in and out of empty rooms
Through the got-one windows.
Steffie lies with the last of the cowboys
Straight up
Ten storeys
Glass streaked with pigeon shit.
Blue façade coming away.
Below delicate cracked concrete cairns
Peeling pipes and filthy coils of wire,
Rusted tether posts and wood chips.
Plastic forks and left-hand Marigolds.
No ball games.
Rose-patterned net curtains flutter
Lazily: no work today.
Front doors left open house
And I swear I heard a cuckoo.
Flayed emulsion, scorched metal walkings
And the flag of St George.
Does anyone hear the clock?

Daisy throws up at the foot of the stairs
Pissed but for the hair of the dog.

Bang out of order.
Woke up asleep in Clark's
Shoe shop doorway.
I know these people
And it's a rude awakening.

The double glazing saves on
You don't hear any ding-dongs going on
Tapping out the time for what seems like hours
Still judge not...
Ends her texts with a flow
Of Emojis.

Higgins I believe she said
You don't talk about that
On the phone.
She was a big lady in the Mothers' Union
Scratches her way along somehow
She came in, oh dear,
Chapter of incidents
Finished with him but it's on again
Don't know who he is
Or where he is.

Grandma doesn't feel safe
In the morning.
I never was like this before,
I must be getting old.
Microwaved, reheated
Crosse & Blackwell
Hearty vegetable soup
And prunes for brekkie.

Geraldine, who sorts my hair,
Does a few hours down there,
What was MacFisheries,

On the till
And him next door
Sorts the tins and veggies
Stacks the shelves after closing.
All pals together.
All the women pinching
Fags and all that.
Marnie Platter, leader of that ring,
Used to do a lot of cooking.
All the ingredients freers.
Thank you very much
Found a dog-end in the pasties,
Sold them up the church
Kept low for a time.
Her husband plays the last part in the band.
The walls are too close together.
He nearly ate a whole loaf of bread and jam
Had to settle on raspberry lifted lightly.
Terrible heart attack. Nearly died.
Lives in the bacon factory that was.
Blind now. His wife can't cope.
The C of E vicar never went near her
When she was that poorly.
The Baptist minister,
No matter what,
Always had a quarter of an hour,
No matter how ill, to chat with Marnie.
Our vicar isn't a good visitor.

Just a minute, I'll put the light on.
A window washed in rain.
One of those days.
Nurse was too busy
Waiting all day long with the door open
Or should we say unlocked?
And nothing happens.

A chatty morning so
Nurse came in during the hairdresser.
Had to come back.
Still nobody came.
A bit straight she was,
Not too much nonsense.
Right, bandages off
Oh, what lovely legs
You look at them
I'm going to put stockings on, she says
We haven't got any bar white stocking.
We'll put on white stockings.
I was thinking its Wednesday.
Melissa can take them off
And put them on again.
You can help them on, far too dry.
Shower day tomorrow.
She put gloves on to peel them over.
Cut the pill in half.
Of course Dr Whatshisname
Has the final say.
Things have changed a bit
Down in the dingle dell surgery.
Ordinary coloured stockings
Are on order
As far as the nurse thinks.
The middle and the end of it.
No good looking at the bad end.
These slippers you're wearing she says,
They're old beyond their years.
They're the only thing that fits me I say,
Ones by the fire are a bit narrow.
White stocking though
Makes me feel more like getting out of the car.

The Eye-aye lads

Have got to accept people
Taking the piss out of them.
A No Person
He's a chatterbox
Wind him up and he's off –
Fighting
Instead of making salad for Susan.
He's always got
People coming to see him,
So get in early.

Last cigarette and fleecy cardigan
The twins sit in their buggy
Chewing dry bread, clutching ABC cubes
As mum offers advice on how to kiss a friend
Before they eat all the chocolate sponge cake.
If things are taken further
Then have a stiff drink at hand
Otherwise it's worse than swallowing quid each oysters.

Big T is followed through the door
By a trio of newly arrived Rawalpindi girls
Shush, cos that's the way, that's the way,
That's the way he likes it.
And he calls it as he sees it.
But you suspect one of them
Is just there to take pictures
On her smartphone.
Or keep an eye on the time.
And, Gordon, who was watching
Through green-tinted sunglasses,
Slips on a discarded johnny.
Serves him right.

Talk to Miss December
Stands at the top of the waterfall

But she's only wearing sunglasses too.
Keep walking.
Despite appearances,
There's nothing for you here.

Your dad walked out,
He didn't say why
Just: "That's what I want to do today."
He's got a duty
At the church at the top of the hill.
At some point I'm going to live next door.

Then there's Hattie,
Walked off the Stannah stairlift,
Bent to pick up a crawliebob,
Best to put it out sooner rather than later,
Next thing she knows flat on the landing
Kissing the carpet.
Hugging the wall.
Used her Lifeline SOS Pendant alarm
But Sidney was up the Sunday pub.
Don't ring Mrs Clutterbuck,
She's in her eighties,
She won't pick me up
But they did.
And her husband came trailing after.
So had to call a nurse,
The ambulances were busy
But she didn't want one anyhow.
The nurse if she called her Hattie once
She called her Hattie forty times.
Drove her spare.
Got hold of the zimmer and walked away.
She really ticked the boxes.
Of course, she hadn't got no keys,
Had to arrange to deliver them.

Back down there
Messing around,
Then this.
Then there you are,
She shut every light out.
Oh, for goodness sake go.
Got up the morning
Parked the zimmer miles away.
Rang his nibs: I'll be in after breakfast.
What a start.
He doesn't know what he doing.
Shall I phone Stella?
Shall I phone Stannah?
Shall I phone Sheila?
I was so tired.
And I was too.
Look at the time.
I didn't want to be black blobbed.
I should have screamed at her,
I hope I never see her again.
You can't win.
You never saw such a palaver
Holding a raincoat over her head.
The first church goers just home.
She had all the chat
Which is normal for herself.
Made a spectacle of ourselves.
Same again tomorrow?
Wait and see.

Abdullah walked
Armed with a green water pistol.
Stole mother's jewellery.
Poke his eye out.
Get a fucking cat,
Get rid of the bird crap.

I hate this place,
I can't leave this place.
No one likes her.

Hickey walked, half in and half out.
Hickey got an eviction notice.
Where are you?
He screwed it up and gave it me back.
Did everyone hear the clock?

Nuttalls walked back and forth:
"I got four fags to last me out all day.
Three if I give the missus one.
Lily get here now. I don't care
What dreams you've got.
I know you can't wait to get
Those shoes off
And have a good chew."

Laura walked to the post box.
First time ever.
She sent her social worker
Chocolates and a card
When, at last, he took the kids away.

The big man's there.
He's been moved into a hotel
And he doesn't like it.
Wouldn't even have a B&B holiday weekend.
No style. Not fair. Just not fair.
Crow, tail bobbing, sits on the TV aerial:
Liar, liar, liar, liar, liar.

The Christmas lights still up,
A blue reindeer and Santa's ladder.
Only Denis watches

From the darkened kitchen.
More tea. Always tea.
Never coffee.
No junk mail.
Hanging baskets, red hot pokers
And yellow roses.
The pebbledash falls in chunks.
What time is it now?

Woz you there?
Woz you there
When Elan was like chatting shit?
I'm here. I'm here. I'm here.
Suited and booted
Didn't even know the man.

Please close the door behind you!

In easily spotted red shoes
Looking down, don't catch her eye
And, as a backcloth,
Oswald Laurence reminds me to
Mind The Gap.

Tube map and sunglasses,
Nicotine patches and pink lollipops,
Black nail polish.
The women on the underground
Putting on orange make-up,
Clutching their purses.
Coffee and Franz Kafka.
Watch their dark reflections.
The importance is not to be seen
To be looking
Not to seem to be seen.
Translations in Greek.
White umbrella
Not a question of shape or race,
Age or apparel
Even when the carriage empties
At London Bridge or Camden
Eyes move over those that remain
Too quickly.

In the corner,
Pandit Boopendre Chakroborty sits,
Attire - purer white,
Reading Sanskrit.
Invisible. For now.

So the driver says:
Please use all the doors,

They're the same colour.
If you don't like red
We can't help you.

All cases and bags and moving on
Skin faced red from the hot shower
Helen Mary combs her long blonde hair
Then ties it into a small bun.
Brush stray strands.
Her arm pits talced,
Her shoulders set,
Checks herself in the compact mirror
Pops a mint: ready to kiss now.
On a silver chain between her breasts:
An Algerian Love Knot.
Bags packed. No more to be said.
Yellow Selfridge's holdall flows with jumpers
And pastel dresses. She's going finally.
Leaving Putney behind at long last.
Sitting still at the edge of the field.
At times like this her accent returns
Soft country heading west that you enjoy so much.

The Serbians, brothers Zivkovic,
Lean forward
Watching for an opportunity
And, in the meantime,
Show each other their fingernails.
The younger, more impulsive, repulsive -
Sneeze. Looks. Wipes on the seat.
Uncle Enoch pushes pasts swearing happily.
Heidi Shelton liberates puppies from pet shops.
She's out of Holloway now.
What's the word?

On the platform at Clapham North,

(You always have to fight
Through the wind
At Northern Line stations),
A kid is screaming and tugging:
I want my mummy back now.
I want my mummy back now.
Father tries to calm him.
They remain on the middle bench,
The child crying again and again:
I want a lolly pop now.
I want a lolly pop now.

Fat Controller smiles.
The limping pigeon crouches
Between the rails
Watched by the black mice.

Réka Turcan,
Serious brown eyes,
Steaua gold star,
Red and blue shawl,
Ankle length black dress
White ivy
Weaving from the hem,
Places the words –
Part printed, part hand-written,
Sorry to disturb you
No job. No help.
I have two year old son
Thank God, is healthy.
Ask for a little aid
To pay rent, pay heating -
And
Soft Silk tissues
On empty seats.
Walks off. Waits.

Ten seconds. Twenty seconds.
Returns. Takes them up,
Shows them to her audience.
One last chance
In case they are unsure.
Their barely raised heads shake in unison.
Moves to the next carriage.
Won't be back.
There, before Highgate,
A kinder woman buys a packet.
Next
An elderly Trinidadian,
Cloth cap, folded newspaper,
Searches his bag, deep and deeper,
Searching for the secret.
Loose change. Pays.
She waits hands loosely at her side
Turning the packet over and over.
She wants the words back though.
Into the sun,
Gets off at East Finchley.
Closes his bag carefully.
She pauses at the man reading,
The man with long tears
Rolling down his thinning face,
But he knew
And already has tissues today.
How am I? Where am I?
At the wine and somatic solace stage.
The lady opposite,
Wearing a recognisably pink pashmina,
Checks again
That she kept her receipt.
At Finchley Central,
As the doors start to close,
A man jumps on, simply mutters:

Oh, Jesus.
Sits down. Closes his eyes.
The rest of the journey is private.

Joey Foxwell ponders an invitation
To another Mouth Party.
His son swings on the handrails
Annoying Lucie Allen
Who is trying to talk down
Eloise Hodges from today's panic attack.
Salvo Ochoa only has six recognisable hairs
On his whole body.
"Land ahoy, my Lord. Pirates."
His son bounces on the seats.
"What rabbit? Rabbit stew?"
Dances around the pole. Swings to the right.
"Land ahoy, my Lord."

Black Labrador pads past
Through the deep-level
Along curved corridors,
In and out of passageways
Who know where
Passing on.
And the busker sings of daylight:
Fa-fa-fa-fa-fags. Fa-fa-fa-fa-fags.
Fa-fa-fa-fa-fags. Fa-fa-fa-fa-fags.

A good service on all other lines.
Except where the man ran out.
Why? You can't ask him.

"Is this train going to Hammersmith?"
"Can you see it written up there?"
The rest of the trip was
Undertaken in Portuguese.

A much quicker language.
"Se você quiser ver o meu bilhete?"

Akela, blue tie too big for his shirt,
A pocket full of woggles,
Not sure he likes what he sees.
An Indian and an Englishman –
Black leather jackets, matching blue jeans,
Spiked and gelled hair -
Holding hands
Ones right thumb constantly stroking
Over the other's hand,
A rhythm across his knuckles.
- Can I get you something for your hands?
From Archway to Kings Cross, St Pancras
He strokes his hand,
The other rests his head on his shoulder
Just before their stop
He kisses him on the cheek
Night-long, day-long stubble.
Stroking. Kissing him on the cheek.
- Where are we going tonight?
Akela, relieved to get off at Euston.
Jenny worries about too much jam
Leaking out of the sponge.
Should have put a sharp knife
Through it. Broken the heart of
Raspberry jam. Far too much.
Boyfriend, arm around her neck,
Laughs too widely.
Jenny Crossland, still bothered.

Turnpike Lane -
Korean teenager:
Can we all say Amen?
She doesn't ask again.

So the driver says:
I do hope the train's going
    in the right direction for you.

Always another stop
Always another question.
What happens here?
Wide-eyed Skender
Woke up in a shock,
Won't take his new daddy's hand.

On towards Old Street
Four twenty-somethings.
When they booked the tickets
Sally said to the man:
As close to the front as possible
Want to see every detail
When Robbie takes his kit off.
So we're sat in row D.
Back to last night evening:
He didn't do anything
Really disappointed
Came round for five minutes
Thinks us is really important.
"Got the tickets Kay?"
Rachel is not listening.
Gold cross-strap, plaited sandals,
Copper blonde beehive
Falling undone at the seams.
Blue-nailed fingers
Pull at the hem of her jumper.
Feels bad about last night
What Kay did to Melissa.
Feels bad now. Too late now.
Was funny then.

"So what we seeing exactly?"
"You know like a Christmas fair thing,
It's like that but for brides."
What?
People can't hear what I'm saying
It's my nose. Essex.
I want to look at the invitations.
Rachel thinks:
When I was fifteen I wrote a list
Things I need to start looking at.
Literally so nervous.
Took a travel sickness tablet
Popped one in her champagne.
She'll be at work now.
What do I say if I ring her?
I hope it wasn't too painful?
You can still pretend, can't you?

Half an hour to midnight
Empty ticket hall,
Dance of the Sugar Plum Fairy
Echoes down the escalator
Intending to keep who calm?
And an eyewitness,
About whom,
In the few weeks ahead,
The tabloids will infer
Bares an unnerving resemblance
To you, says:
You never know
    what you're going to get
        at stations.

Unease, change carriages
Something not right
Get above ground

Away from the eyes
Eyes that say:
          You have done something
Just because you don't remember
Just because you pretend
Just because you're close to me
Doesn't matter.
Carry on above ground.

Bob's harmonica crashes
Off the white tile walls
As a call goes out for Inspector Sands
On the look out
For all station staff.

Push through the crowd
Out. Out. Out.

Ladies and gentleman
For your own safety
Please stand behind the yellow line.

Mind The Gap, pleads Mr Laurence.

iii

All day breakfast
Two eggs, bacon, sausage
Talking of strawberries
Put a cloth on the table.

Phone ringing down the hall
How do you know that?

What colour's your hair?
Excuse me, could I have apple crumble
                        and ice cream please?
The coconut sponge and custard?
Last night my mum:
You need to sign something
That's what money is for?
Cherry?
I'm not starting on you
Just want fried onion.

One tea. One coffee
He's here?
Yeah, he's here.
Crusty roll with bacon
And sliced mushrooms.
Tea as it comes.

 - How many sugars you want?
Make it a threat.
You don't want to see
Me in high heels
Moving furniture around
At two in the morning.
Coming home from the weekend
With a virus going round.

My saving grace
Is the clocks finishing.
The priest won't look
At children out of wedlock.
Nice piece of weather.
Take a sachet
Put your own sugar in.
Happy Days.

- Chicken and mushroom pie, carrots.
Gravy on top.

I don't want to be invited.
Another black coffee.
Morning. It's too loud.
No butter.
So where's your brother today?
He's a good boy, I tell you.
Never again.

Egg and bacon
Scrambled egg
No fat on the bacon
I'll tell you the price
And you'll give me extra bacon
And I'll not wear a shirt
And the clasped hand tattoo
          over my heart remembers her
And I'm observing a minute's silence
          at noon
And the boy sits
And the door swings
And the riddles fall flat
And he crosses out the swear words.

- Chicken and cabbage.

28

Don't touch. Cabbage or broccoli.
The road-sweeper sits by his broken brush
Slurping noodles, weeping and losing interest.
Got attacked for a ham and cheese omelette.
The Greek came storming out,
Apron flapping,
Squirts HP sauce,
Southpaw with the spatula,
Salt to the left, pepper to the right
Big plate and hot beverages.
Slap not the old boxing, mate.
The Polish waitress:
"Is everything for you fine?"

My gran says it's a filthy habit
Eating them sugar snap peas from the pod.
You might get a maggot.
You'd see a maggot, I says.

Mum counting out her money,
Dad eating bread and dripping
Corned beef roll. Thank you. Twice.
The Sun tells me Jez can do it.
You're like an old woman
The way you treat your toast.
Always with a doggy bag
Don't know how she gets on
When there's gravy.

Toby's job is to eat the misorders
Buttered white instead of brown,
Two sugars instead of plain,
Over hard instead of runny sunny.
Sitting there making the place
Busy and keen.

- Pineapple upside-down.
Hot, with custard.

Job weighing sparrows.
The emergency doughnut,
Still sitting, watching jam bleed,
Protected under a saver dome.
Plastic not glass: Just in case.

Bang. Bang. Bang.
Mickey shoots the staff
With his aluminium walking stick
Nine, nine, nine
Sal calls the Bill.
Happy days.
Luckily Wiktoria speaks no English
Mixes up flat bread and bloomer,
Confuses salad cream
For mayonnaise.
Monday?
Tuesday better day.

All the trimmings
All desserts with custard
All home cooked.
Reading it upside down.
Cheers mate scrape the black
Off the burnt toast,
Egg swims in yellow oil,
Black pudding dry as dust.
The chef watches Loose Women:
Waits for the rush.
Andreas peels oranges with a hunting knife.

In the corner,

Walter has had thirty years of it.
Doesn't want to talk about it
And talks till twilight.
You do keep on, don't you?
She gets under his skin
Chips creep off the plate
Corned beef without the carrot
Tea – find you sugared it twice
That Saturday breakfast was shit.

Fill your plate.
Dean dreams of about
Thirty rashers of crispy bacon
If only he had the teeth to chew them.
Finish your breakfast
Haven't got all day.

Outside on the zig-zag lines
The ambulance is still parked
Blocking the traffic lights
Because he kissed her
As they crossed the road.
The scene marked in white powder.

That kind of thing
Leaves a bad taste in your mouth.

iv

Pyjamas and dressing gowns,
The Smoking Circle take the air,
Wheelchairs and saline IV-drips,
A slow infusion hung
On rattlesome-tettersome four-legged poles,
Talk about the old times.
Inside, on ill at ease steel chairs,
The bouncebackers & Hasselhoffs,
The PFOs, Tough sticks & hippos
Count the four hours.

Pass familiar doorways
Ultrasound. Oncology.
"Have you been weighed yet, sir?"
Outpatients Clinic A.
No red sticker
So take a number.
General 409.
Just behind the Glucose Kid.
Sometimes numbers may be
Called out of turn.
Read about the bird flu.
They have different ways.
The doctor has about two days
Off sick a week.
Number called.
Have you been fasting?
Is it Ramadan?
Sharp scratch.
See your GP in one week.

The orange shirts push Mr Myers,
Arm-banded Intervene Adult,
Back and along

Each time he passes
Frailer, thinner, apologetic
For all the bother this causes.
The wives tap out Morse
With their sticks and canes –
Cover us in warm stones.
The red-rimmed vandal
Cuffed to the officer
Wants more snacks and the woman
In the oxygen mask says:
Everything's just fine.

Palmer Lawful Lynton,
Part Jamaican carpenter,
Part British socialist,
Marched with the panther Darcus Howe,
Read as much as Stuart Hall time permitted,
Dreams still of Oxbridge spires, Churchill,
Shakespeare and the Queen,
Will not have another pill,
Refuses the clutches of Donepezil.
Remembers four decades back
Uncle Calvin
When they opened him up
His no longer delicate insides
Organs rock-hardened by chalk.
Palmer Lawful Lynton says:
God will take me
On a different path.
Man-made time,
Made a lot of it.
Will still taste the tang
Of ackee and saltfish.
The quality of my story
Left behind
Will not end on a handful of pills.

Are you dealing with doctors again?
Sarah Tyler texts:
I can't have children.
Guess we weren't going to anyhow.
Don't trust doctors.

How are you?
Why did they take so much blood out?
Do you know where this is?
Still-shocked children
Reach for a hand
You're not my child
So I have to share fairly.

The Mother:	If I died in the lounge I'd be comfortable.
The Father:	And then you'd remember I put you there.
The Son:	Comfortable.

And two by two,
The Filipino nurses take the temperature
The old fashioned way. Nil by mouth.
And two by two
The Trinidadian nurses make the beds
With perfect hospital corners.
And two by two,
The Ghanaian nurses moisten lips
And administer saliva spray with care.
And two by two,
The Irish nurses pour extra strong, four sugars tea
And present a pink straw to drink it through.
And two by two,
The Zimbabwean night nurses turn the patient religiously
On the hour but not always into the best position.

And two by two,
The Thai nurses unlock the cabinet, extract the pills and
          potions
And serve ice-cold, two inch long chocolate éclairs.

And lastly, not leastly, four by four the consultants walk past
Come to ask the questions and tick the charts
See: minimized thigh sores, eradicated heel blisters.
Treatments to help the medicine go down in a hassle-free
          way.

The Whisper Ward
Head scarves and smiles
Free sandwiches & toffee yoghurt
Testing chairs
Arm in a bucket of warm water
Bring out your veins.
When's the next injection?
The regulars start talking
Freezer boy. Painter-decorator.
Ex-offender. Jubbly orange woman.
Leafleting. Saturday job.
Print buyer.
I never really had a job.
Find yourself three floors up
Simply watching clouds.
Thinking about
Another friend on the missing list.
Then my wife said:
How long..?
Yet an orderly interrupts
More forms need filling. DNR.

Breathe through your tube
Into your stomach
Never going to talk again.

The pain melts skin-deeper
You are beautiful deeper still.
Comb-over yawns,
X-ray can wait another while.

A mother screams:
That's my son. He's dying.
And no one can do anything.
And no one will tell me anything.
The truth cuts through conversation
And everyone tries to scratch
A way through the windows.
This is the worst thing.
Really.
The worst thing in the world.

Suddenly the grey corridor empties.
The chapel is closed for relocation.
The ward accessible for
Immediate family members only.
Anguish soaks into the grey speckled lino.
In a futile side ward
A man lays Tarot cards
On a bare desk
And whispers the numbers.
Tries to work out why his trousers are wet.
Ted Cottle hopes to see Thursday.
The doctor smiles.
White walls
Metronomic alarm warns
You'll never reach
Receding exit doors.
Blue surgical gowns
Flapping on a washing line
Delicately tended by Abena.

Just up from the Majors.
Third floor tighter spaces.
Here to make you feel better.
Couldn't think
Where we were this morning.
Words spill,
Hanging loose.
Hello, my name is Mary,
I'll be your nurse for the day.
Have you had lunch?
Steak & kidney pie?
Crackers in obdurate cellophane?
What time is it?
Say: Mama
Say: Fifty-fifty
Say: Huckleberry
Say: Baseball Player
Say: Tip-top
See how your lips work.
I hate bedpans.
NBM.
I'll be honest with you,
We can't find your medical notes
But we can find you.
Put you on a trolley
And promise they'll only leave you for a minute
And in an hour and a half
You still believe them.
Foul-mouthed old dregs next to me
Had to keep the curtain pulled.
Jane comes about, takes some bloods –
Which arm?
The promise of an aspirin suppository.
Won't talk about the steak & kidney pie.
The sky is a creeping magenta
And all the leaves are blank.

Water moves too fast
For my mouth.
Lauren, dark green nursing assistant
And part-time ALCOHOL ADVISOR
Comes with a bowl of warm water.
Fluids finished, warm water,
Clearing the sleepy-dust, warm water.
- Mrs Fisherton, do you know where you are?
Bed-rest and just a bit of rolling now.
I've seen things
And everything is so beautiful.
Where are we?
Evangeline: there's a nicer shop
Full of nicer things.
Do you like beef? Good,
That's what I like to hear.
Have you ever had tapioca?
Not very exciting.
She's diabetic.
Put unsugared jam in it.
Like eating frog spawn
With no cherry on top.
I'll have one part of a parsnip instead.
Bev frowns – the noise:
The alarms, the bells, the ringing.
Draws herself deeper still
And tries to listen to her programmes.

Sprinkle perfume on the sheet.
Take you out of hospital.
Get you back into a bit of a pattern
If possible.
- Good morning, Mrs Perera,
You're looking nice tonight.

My husband on his horse back in Cornwall.

I'm going away with the fairies
They dressed me in clothes that aren't mine.
Find what's lurking inside me.
Four blouses in that closet that are a shame.
See what it does. We'll all fall down.
I wouldn't be seen dead in those clothes really.
Came and took me from the room in the middle of the night.

Now only Avril watches -
The ballerina displays attitude,
Sorry for the things she's done,
The possible lovers who don't talk enough,
The language falls away, leaving them,
The Maltesers roll across the table,
Past books never read,
Off on to the hospital floor
But she doesn't care.
You can't eat these now, Avril
You know where they've been.
Where are your slippers?
Why are you hugging them so tightly?
I think we should pop you in a cupboard
You're so wibbly-wobbly.

The paper & sweet biscuit man arrives after lunch
The Sunday Mail is the Tuesday Mail
And the news is stale.
Vanessa cries as they slide her away –
She doesn't want to go
Into the unknown.
Orlena's problem was always the diced carrots.
Little Stephanie is in the isolation room
Just got her to put a mask on
For handing over.

Rosemary, Rosemary, can you wake up for me?

Rosemary? Rosemary? Can you open your eyes?
Estella, can you look at me? Can you look me in the face?
Olive, have you got the magic touch?
Audrey, would you like a bit of brightness in your life?
Phyllis, are the doctors being too gentle?
Joan, get you up and get you dancing, shall we?

Sigh and the constant stare
In bed-land.

Bed 2: I didn't get my cup of tea.
Bed 4: Tea?
Bed 2: Yes please.
Bed 3: I'm as dry as a fish.
Bed 7: Hello, I'm looking for someone
Bed 2: I haven't had my tea yet.
Bed 8: Can I have my bed back? Can I have my bed?
Bed 2: Did I hear about a drink? I haven't had mine yet.
Bed 7: Tea lady. Do you take sugar in your tea?
Bed 8: A quick supper last night.
Bed 1: Slept like a saint.
Bed 3: But you didn't sleep last night.
Bed 6: Or the night before.
Bed 4: Keep yourself covered up sweetheart.
Bed 2: Put a tube in so I can have some hot soup.
Bed 10: Tell my husband I love him very much.
Bed 8: Can I have my bed?
Bed 1: My chocolate biscuit.
Bed 8: Can I have my bed back?
Bed 2: Did I hear tea?
Bed 5: I'll go to the machine. They do make coffee at the
        machine.
Bed 1: Watch your hands.
Bed 5: Watch your chocolate biscuits.
Bed 2: I don't know why I didn't have any tea.
Bed 7: Dinner smelt delicious. Shame how it ended.

Bed 6: I can stand to a wall of pots and pans.
Bed 4: I want to wonder and get up and go.
Bed 8: I want my handbag. How far are we going to go?
Bed 7: Do you know where you are?
Bed 2: There's a lot of people missing in here.
Bed 3: Ron, tapped his dominoes on the table wood every
     time he laid.
Bed 7: So did my brother-in-law with the Scrabble. You
     wouldn't believe the language he came out with.
Bed 6: Why peaches again?
Bed 1: Peaches are cheap.
Bed 8: Don't move me to a side room.
Bed 5: We know what ends in a side room.

Senior Sister Maplesden: Do you know what they're saying?
Staff Nurse Rathbone: Can't quite make it out.
HCA Davison: Don't you hear? They are singing.

Hospital heat seeps through.
Nothing that I could have done.
Pull the tubes from your arm.
Tear the dressings from the stitches.
Peel off your snowflake print gown.
Why? They don't fit right. Feel right.
One of us is going quietly crazy
And it's not you. I can't stop.
Infection burns lucidity soundlessly.
A fine rain falls
As the patient behind the curtain
Drops her warmed milk.
Where are we walking to this time?
Through alleyways, across broken glass
Out in the drizzle, stepping over bridges.
Do you understand me the way you did?

Rosemary: Can I have a cup of tea?

Estelle: When was the promise of tea?
Olive: Bring me a tea, I'll be so grateful
Audrey: Mix it with Nutilis.
Phyllis: One blue spoonful.
Joan: One pink spoonful.
Lisa: One green spoonful simply for luck.
Natalie: Tea as tar.
Nicola: No, no, no. Yes. Tea as thickening treacle etc, etc.
Dawn: Stirred with a wish and a prayer.
Constance: What happened to my cup of tea?
SN Rathbone: Soon.
Caroline: Have you brought the tea?
Helen: I am never quite sure when soon actually is.

Debbie: Knock, knock – here's the tea.

In the side-room
Everybody can hear you scream
In the side-room
Boy does Polly-Anna scream.
In the side-room
- Help me. Please, please help me.
In the side-room
The blinds are drawn.
In the side-room
The disappearing refuse to stay silent.

(Ward Sister Willett
Pulls the cracker,
Wears the green paper hat,
Pockets the quartet of marbles and asks:
"What do you call a penguin in the Sahara Desert?")
Penguins queuing in the cafeteria,
Penguins at the bus stop,
Penguins turning my pockets inside out.
I see them as I return home

And you indulge me. I can't stop.
("Lost").

Just hold your hand
And sit there
In silence
After visiting hours.
The nurse draws the curtain round us
Into our own world.

Shout:	"Where are you?"
Scream:	"Where are you?"
Weep:	"Please come back."
Mutter:	"Thank you for everything."

The women have all gone back to bed.
- Can I please get out of here?
- Don't forget: accidents happen.
- Don't forget... We'll all fall down.

Orange balloon tumbles into traffic
Escapes out between
The gap in the sickly turquoise railings.

Out, into the rest of the world.
A line of cars,
All painted vermillion,
All served with penalty change notices.
Yellow privet hedges,
Rose buds,
Weeds climb through crazy paving.
The lollypop man watches the new ones
Go about their business.
All money but no manners.

Help me finger-drawn faces

Children spike haired, tongues out
Across the condensation passenger windows
Approaching cold front
With a mixed bag of impacts.
Increased chances of rain.

The alcoholic nudist fishmonger
Knocks on another door
Asking for money.
He has lost everything
And now his mind
Wants to play those tricks.
Cooked the M&S Cod
And white sauce
Fifteen minutes –
The specified time.
Stirred it out of the oven.
He could hear the ice cracking
In the bottom of the potato.
If he gets the collywobbles
He'll know what it was.
He knew the fish-man at Tooting
He could make the hake and haddock
Talk back in Welsh and Cockney,
He could make the crabs bubble
And he could help the cuttlefish
Analyse their own Rorschach blots
And sign away their names in cursive script.
He didn't make it.
Nothing's the same anymore.
No one knows
The life of a fishmonger.
Added to everything,
Can't get the stink out.

Lili Rouge

Sits in her wheelchair,
Left on the apex of the railway bridge
Enjoying a walnut whip:
Biting the crisp chocolate top,
Nut first,
Licking out the cream,
Watching the heavy traffic.
Worse each day.
Listening to Talk Radio,
Waiting for a push
To the corner of College Road.
Who left her there in the first place?

The Poundshop: a horrible place
People pushing by
To put themselves nearer the window
I hate Poundland.
No one touched nothing neither
Christine didn't take no notice.
What good's a cut-out policeman?
Had to wait for the security man to come
But they can't hear everything
And she had two twenties.
All precisely folded in thirds
So you could see the Queen.
I hate Poundland.
They've got good stuff though
Clumby needs his chocolate.
Don't be shy.
Come on in, dear.
Take a look.
You don't have to buy
I'll take your money another day.

Millicent Moss
Reads the used matchsticks.

Derek won £25
She won £25
Don't think Michelle ever won
I think Cathy's in the Euro
What have we done with the money?
New numbers
Far too easy to win
Who's still in?
Thought there were twelve of us
Around the table.
Were. But look who's gone
In just the last year.

Up the steep steps.
White door
Flat 2, 3, 4.
Marked in DIY gold labels.
Nobody can find Flat 1 now
But they can smell the proper fish & chips.
Quarter past eight came
And went
It was there once.
Across the lights
The Specials break up a rumpus
At the Peace ceremony.
Everyone wants to be in the photo
With the local politician.
The pickie-pockies
Bump and slide on the periphery.
Nobody wants to be the first
To light a candle.

Red Pledge mug Number 4: Immigration
Wrapped up warm in the loving embrace
Of an Indian princess
Nanny King wouldn't recognise the place

Now
She took flight to the Kentish coast
Not a moment too soon.
Letterboxes, my niece calls them.
Struggle across at the lights
Battle prams and pushchairs.
The wheelchairs brakes are old
And the man selling peacock feathers
Won't help for asking.
I know everyone
But they don't like you.
No place for foreigners.
The Poles come and take all the jobs
They say.
We have enough friends, they say.
In Zurich you can swim in the river,
Smile a little.
It's not pretty around this time.
What's up little pumpkin?
No one is called this anymore
We have enough Fatimas in the world.
It's beautiful but.. everyone is called Ananya
It's fine to call her Kheezran.
So, are you hoping to
Go back home now?
It's time.
I wish I could stay forever.
But I don't speak
Farsi, or Hindi, or Gujarat.
It's crazy
The Broadway: you have to see it once
Like Vegas, you only have to see it once.
Walking here is
Like running the Great Wall of China
All uneven steps.
Seraphima plays the harmonica

And is silly with her little friends.
Happy is her first abstract word.

The beauty parlour is boarded up
A sign saying beware corgi on duty
Torn in the breeze.
On his hands and knees,
Franklin brushes up the privet leaves
Glances at the woman
High heels at the wrong time of day
To walk to the station, hope she's not stoned.
Street signs obscured by white paint
Pigeons wrestle pizza slices school dinners
Cross the road at a dangerous bend
Offices. Windows broken.
The butcher sits in the back room
Counting leaflets.
Spooney's House, faces ripped away,
He'll happily give you
A Church Street Special.
Music boarded up. Neon shattered.
The Tryst. Knotweed growing from the upstairs window sill
Too blind to tell go or stay
The Mohican with the ring through his nose
Sighs. Nothing to say
Black-hooded, skull and crossbones.
Stacey runs the up side down the escalator
Her red Sloane Square sandals blur
Excuse me, I'm going the wrong way.
The paparazzi take flash shots of handbags.
The woman on the tandem licks her lips
Who's to tell what catches her eye
Ceramic macaws, yellow seated pigs
In Paradise Walk.
Where, even now, far too late,
For the covers to come on
The mower goes back and forth

Twenty-two yards in, twenty-two yards out.
The streets smell of custard creams.
None of it is pretty.

Wayne Wilson.
He's got two names by all and sundry.
One we'll talk of,
The other:
Find out by yourself
In laybys and warm bonnet clearings,
In the cul-de-sac and bent over dead-ends.

So, the one we'll talk of –
Put It Back Wayne.
Nicks to order
Susses out the CCTV
Fancy a cashmere scarf from M&S?
Choice of five. Herringbone or print?
On first name terms
With checkout girls and security guys
Goes all the way back to
Ferrero Rocher? You can't fake quality.
Manuka honey from Sainsbury's?
One jar or three? Organic?
Sandwiches at lunch? A drink with that?
A sorcerer's finger tricks
Below the counter.
Birthday List. Christmas List.
Shopping List. Wedding List.
I am a true artist, here's your rake
He says.

The Turkish barber never speaks
Above a whisper
But he soon learns
What he needs to know

The blade is cut-throat fresh
And the thumb and forefinger
Massage the eyes and throat
Expertly.

Jazzman has two hats
And a bag of Chinese dumplings.
Kills three or four birds
With one stone.
The ants are carrying it off.
The supermarket is marking down
Red labels.
Go over in my slippers,
A lazy uncle
Visiting once a month
Handing out sweets.
A nice lady came round
Told you the names of the pies
Available.
If you're a man,
Wear a hat.
You're still going to die
But at least go with dignity.
Jazzman took me to one side
To explain the laws of
Marmite toast.
It's the warm sauce
That scrubs up feelings.
The zest for life.
It soaks up all the alcohol,
It soaks up the desire for life.
Then first thing
Go out stealing silver top
Or, at a pinch, blue top
When the milkman is up stairs.

There are so many of them
Sorry, madam, it is not for sale.
Girl wails, shows a mouthful
Of barely chewed Tuc.
Why do you have to cry?
Looking at the migrant in his raincoat
On a hot summer's day.
Isn't that enough to make you laugh?
The returned empty spinster
Cares for three legged frogs
And recently orphaned tadpoles.
Ruddy faced men,
Kodak instamatics around their necks,
Snap at women in knitted hats.
The door is open,
You can see the clock
And the umbrella stand
But the gate is locked.
Meet at the statue.
There are still a few strawberries left.
Welcome back, sir.

vi

Ring the bell.
Tell Krishna I am here.
The day drags on
Walk into the Temple
Which should by rights be shut now.
Even uninvited,
I remove my shoes
And enter through the right hand doorway
Gent Sabhu.

The orange collection tins
Hang in plain sight.
A bucket full of coconuts.
Bananas and apples
Placed for the Gods.

Come to this:
Stealing bananas from a temple.

Shree Ganpatiji –
The white elephant
Covered in red roses.
Ganesh
First on the guest list,
Invited to all the best parties,
All the finest weddings,
Bringing the gift of success.

Then I see him.
He walks around the Gods
Three times.
Three times round
Shree Swaminarayan Bhagum
- the centre of everything.

The Pujari.
Bare feet
Red dot
Short, greying hair
White robes
Eyes black
Looking in to the soul.

He knows I've been eating onions.
Onions alter the mind,
Make you do the unexpected,
Give your mind excuses.

Which God will you pray to?
Which do you believe in most?
Any God will help you.
A humble request.
I believe you need
To remove obstacles.
Studying at the murti,
I saw you pause at Ganesh.
Speak with him.
I saw you recoil
At Sheshnag,
Floating on an ocean of milk:
Let him guide you
Show you the truth that remains
Even when you believe time is over.

Above all there is
Krishna
Kill all the devils
Drive them out. God comes in the form of Krishna
But each God has importance
Blue has no mixture.

It is his own. Krishna was born on a dark night
When lots of bad things arise
He will come again.
With supernatural powers
Which we are unable to describe.

Offer food first
After bath
Offer flowers
Offer fruit
Live with pure devotions.

Don't go empty handed.
The priest gives me fruit
Bananas, apples, rock sugar.
Drink the water.

At the break of day
As you put your first foot down
Pray to the goddess Earth.
As you step on the Earth
Forgive me stepping on you.
In the centre of your two eyes
Is the God.

Donation for Cow.
Cows are special
Give us the milk
Ladies are in its body
Mother of us all
Earth are mothers
Rivers are mothers.
Today is the new moon day.
Amavasya
Take holy bath
Take bath for purity

There are many rivers
Out there.
Find one
Head there
And take that bath.
Don't have to go to the
Ganga.
Don't have to go to the
Shipra
    (although you will).
This is a chance.
Go to the river.

So a bare six months later,
With the Russians destabilizing
And the Chinese island building,
The middle fell apart. Sold off.

The stadium all shut down,
The dogs have gone feral,
The pitch full of used cars.
Link fencing and barbed wire.
Keep in? Keep out?

Now those who were excluded
Meet at the market.
The dealers and collectors
Have been and gone with the night,
Just dawn rummagers left
Picking through tangled vestments
And standard sheer denier stockings.

Wander
As long as you like
For a pound
Take your ticket.

Two Sues together
Won coupons on Heart FM
For a Kate Bush tribute act.
Never been so excited.

On the floor
All I see are blue sandals
Of which we get many.

Tipped his mother out

Nasty piece of work.
Dolphin glass clock
Stuck at 12:37.
Frosted frogs
And singing china pigs,
Fossils, crystals.
Browse.
Invest the baby's savings.
Four glass ballerinas
£48 the set (or best offer).

Flushed Mr Punch,
Yellow hair,
Red & blue frilled collar,
Grins at their plight. Hard times
Over the past nineteen months.

Too thin men carry odd chairs
Chung down Pick Your Own raspberries:
"You were supposed to give me today
Eighty quid.
That's the situation."

The chain man is following
The unsuspecting
Each step links rattle
Plastic bags wrapped around his wrists
Smuggled in by Poles
The stories of the gas are his.
The children roll in dust.

"Two pound each or five for the three
That's making them very cheap."

Rusted pails, a pound for two.
Kitchen foil. Earthenware jars.

Impossible to separate
Everything for sale.
50p on the floor.
Three cups, two saucers.
Half an array of chipped antlers
A set of army fatigues.

"That's right. You're back for it."
"Really? Am I?"
Punters skirt the puddle
Drowned green
Plastic bags floating.

Holding hands
With a chipped-finger mannequin?
That's a pound. Folded curtains? A pound.
A blue LK Bennett Detroit wedding dress? A pound.
A pile of 1970s & 80s diaries? A pound.
A collection of 1990s & 2000s photographs? A pound.
Out-and-out love? A pound.
Another chance? Withdrawn from sale.
Happy ever after? No call for it in these parts.
Time? Ah, already gone. Already sold.
If only you'd come down to Summerstown
In March when you first felt it.
Keep the change.

Beefeater offers beans on toast
Big cup of tea. 60p.
Sean Connery and Clint Eastwood
Watch over the diners.
Can we play with the wrestlers yet?
Kane and Batista tag team.
Fyffes banana boxes abandoned,
Rolling cans and broken glass.
On an upturned apple cart,

Four jockeys, old now by years,
Much anticipated in the good book,
Deal the cards.
"You can be the North
And myself the South."
Hold the two of clubs.
Old Bill East goes for the biscuits,
Rich tea is all that's left.

In the far corner the music plays
Layla, extended version,
And you know who that's for.
Cos I smile now
And see the future wide open.
She's sitting at the back
Sipping latte or wine and staying quiet.

"A jacket. Say two pounds."
Soap stone pirate heads
East Anglian saucer maps
Mirrors that reflect the sky.

In the other corner of the car park.
"Are you watching for the dogs, Mr Toogan?
For the dogs?"
Faelyn sits on the outside wall,
Finishes her strawberry-seasoned e-ciggie.
Somebody's son,
Chicken Kiev breath,
But she'll kiss him anyhow
Cos he asked.
Backstreet behind the station:
Do you see the joke?

- Fancy seeing you here?
My ex- with her new

Her new my best man
My best man has been here before
Back in the day.
Then...
        he said he fancied Bonnie Langford
And Barry agrees with him.
You said you fancied
The pretty woman in Purrfect Pixz
The lithe, giggly one,
The Likes Cake & Tea one
Who turned a blind eye
And always printed six interesting extras.

She'd have slapped you up bruv.
What ever happened to her?
What were you thinking?

- Fancy seeing you here?
Too many questions.
(Said she was becoming a cat woman.
Her up the road.
Assumed really where is this leading to?
Lives on a hill.
Happy to be unloved.
Live in the sticks).
- Stop giving someone your life.
(Step back. Black & white cat
Sits at the window looking out at the road,
The countryside.
Scrap.
Round here).
- Would you like to pop in?
The knob on the bannisters
Painted with a clown face.
- Tea or coffee?
- Milk and sugar?

(I'll have tea).
- That'll keep you going.

- Cake with this then?
(Talk about country cats,
 You live in a nice area.
 Not like the sticks.
 No snakes.
 A ginger tom patrols
 The back fence.
 Cats cure sleepless nights).
- That's you weak bladder.
- What were we talking about?
Look at that!

- Who is paying for the cake?

Shirtless in my yellow home
Fishing into the face of a red snapper.
A plate of awkward oddments
& uncomfortable attachments
Take it all home in a green wheelbarrow.
The Warning Guard Dogs
Sign hangs by one plastic clip
On a collapsed chain-link fence.
A row of whisky bottles, drunk clear,
Line the bricked wall.
Stools upturned on ringed tables
As hustler hoovers:
Who wants a tray of table lamps
Cheaper than chips?
Fondue sets, mock crystal candle sticks,
Bed-bound cardigans and remnants
Only one vanishing owner.

Against site rules

Finger-tips rub the rust
Beneath the ill-fitting bonnet
Of a car of two colours.
The smaller- town dealer offers generously
A warrant4Life,
4Lunchtime
Whichever is sooner.

"We haven't got much time."
A line lost in the breeze.
A bronze pixie blows at the rain
£1 wrist watches.
"Where are you gonna spend it?"

Everything just one price.
Come down here and sell.

"He was a very nice man."
Solitaire. Two karat diamond
Selling buying, talking selling?
Talking two thousand.

Two sewing machines
And a goldfish in a gilded frame.

"How are you? Alright?
How's your mum?"

The lorry ladies are getting bolshie:
Sack us. Go on, I dare you
You can't get girls in for
Love nor money.

You not allowed to
Leave any rubbish or
Unsold items in the car park.

"Cheers, John."
You won't see one again
No fighting.
More naked Barbies, left shoes
Afro junk, wood polish.

"You want to give me £8?
How are you? Blessed?"
Box of ladies wigs. "Take care, madam."

"Talk to the man with the chemise."
Special price.

"Anything a quid:
You've got to look, surely?"
Sun faded paintings
All colours blue.
Cleared furniture -
Blistered veneer.

"I have a ticket."
"Once you're out, you're out."
"I have this ticket."
"That's the rule."

Fu moves the chess pieces.
Wait here until you are required.
Jacqui will dance with you Cat Daddy
Because that's in the contract.
And Soufiane will sell you lengths
Of hand sewn Moroccan carpets
And sit as we play IT across the city.
The Dobermans sleep soundly tonight.

"Every day's

A good 'en, isn't it?"

"Coming back again, love?"

Stamp your hand.
"You're always welcome here."

viii

Hard times
Over the past nineteen months
I'm not out
Seven days a week
I go to a disabled friend's
Twice a week.
Or
I sleep in the market doorway.
Went to the Centre
Got rid of the day
We'll give you floor space,
They say.

Crouches against the glass
Outside the newsagents
Got no home
Carrying one banana.
Searches each pocket for a lighter.
Click of crutches
Towards, right past, fades.

People come past
You clock 'em
They talk to you
If you've got a bowl or hat
Check what's in the hat
Check what's in the bowl
Grab it and gone
By the time you're up
Vanished
All for a quid or so.

An extra fifteen or twenty beggars
Out on a Saturday.

Faces not familiar
Which you don't see all week
Not genuine
Make their bed up in a doorway
But I'm still there five in the morning
When they've long since buggered off
Back and snug.

My name's Dave.

Best meal a Gregg's meal
Steak and cheese
Or sausage roll.
Friday or Saturday
You get people come along
Beggar spotting Friday night
Saturday night along Queen Street
Here they call your name
Call you names
Throw things at you.
Throw a handful of chips
Coins, cold cans at us.
And obviously
When it rains as well.
Bastards.
I tell 'em
They're one step from me
If their missus kicks 'em out.
They'll be next door
Outside Morrison's.

Split up with my missus
I met her she had two kids
One of our own came along
I was working away, see.
I was roadie-ing. Setting the stage.

She wanted me to stop in town
Then the baby came along
It was: I don't want you gone
The most I was gone for was
Twenty-eight days
Then it was a weekend
At the end of the day
I only worked a couple of days a week.
How could that support us?
Three months later we were split
All through work
I left her with the house
…and the kids.

Nineteen months.
I'm out in the night
I sit opposite Santander.
Or near McDonalds.
The first burger I get
She gets.
She gets the meat,
The bun goes to the birds.
The second burger
She gets half
I have a half.
Feed her first
At the end of the day
It ain't her fault.

Had a flat for a while
Landlord and Landlady split up
It was the Landlady's house
She wanted me gone
She hired a guy
Paid him fifty notes
To get me out of the house.

Broke my jaw.
Lucky he didn't kill me.
Obviously I moved out
He was an ex-boxer,
Fit as a fiddle
But I lost everything.
Police did nothing
I knew if I spoke
He'd come looking for me
I didn't bump into him since.
He was a nutter.
He kicked off fights,
Punched out
Off-duty police officers.

Women are the kindest.
I don't blame no woman
For anything.
Charmaine comes past
Goes and gets me a Greggs
Some biscuit treats
And all she wants is a hug.
She says: it doesn't cost anything
Only money.
Mrs Platt feeds her
Cooked chicken slices.
She loves chicken,
She'd eat it
Until her belly don't move.
That woman who thought she saw you
She thought you were the soup man
Comes round his morning early
Always vegetable or tomato.
She promised him a slurp
Told her he wouldn't be back.

Bloke with the bag Martin
Got a bull mastiff
With a tongue that long
Way too big for his mouth.
Sammie says: dogs are good
Dogs gets us money.

Worst is how people look at you
I say: have you got the time?
They say: I haven't got any spare
I ain't asking for spare,
Just a note of the time.

The hostel says :
She can't come in here
We don't know you that well
Give her away.
Send her to a Special shelter
Would you give away your kids?
If I leave her
She goes nuts.
The fuss
If I'd been gone a week
She's lost
Wouldn't give her up
She keeps me sane
Gives me a reason to wake up.

Winters.
The wind and the rain
I was out.
Can't do seven days a week
Not now.
Even in a dry enough spot.

Kids are alright now

One of the ones
He was in the Salvation Army
Had an argument in there
Moved into his own pod
He's got psychiatric problems
He flips over something small
He says: if I'm in a bad mood
Let me go out
Then we'll discuss
What needs to be discussed
The woman said no,
So he kicked off.
They want you away
If you've been there x-amount of time
If you've been there too long
They want rid of you.
Floor space for
Six to eight months
Then he got a pod.
All his life inside out ways
And all for just ten minutes
All the shit
For not having ten minutes
Ten minutes wasted arguing
Could have been ten minutes outdoors.

And the Jehovah's asks:
Is the end near?

The ex-wife fell behind,
Ended up in the hostel.
Now she's been rehoused.
She had a couple more kids
After me
Had two more daughters.
Lights of her life.

If you're past here again
Or up at the end of Queen Street
We'll talk some more.

Outside the newsagents
Sits Dave
And a dog called Trixie.
Trixie,
Miniature Jack Russell,
Turned twelve last November
 Hoping I get another.
Good four or five years
Her eyes are a bit off
Same thing, her bladder
That's why I sit her on this towel
Saves getting wet.
Man's best friend without a doubt.

I'll get there in the end
At the end of the day
I look at it
I'm in a better position.

In the world
So many people
Worse off than me.

ix

Magic City with its sordid toy shop
Now wash your hands.
"Have a little look girls and boys."
Toys out the back of the yellow van:
Naked Barbies bend,
Action Man keeps his trousers on.
China dolls with cracked faces
Delicately maim the plastic animals
Pandas, decapitate giraffes
Rhinos: get them before they're gone.
Knitted penguins, blind gold Daleks.
Anyone else for bubbles?

But take yourself
Then to the house.
The bell rings above the door.
Life gets better, don't be scared,
Have a chocolate éclair.
Place a coin in the clown's hand.
Careful, he'll swallow you whole.
Come on in, Sunny Jim.
A snake in the box,
Humpty Dumpty's circus is in town,
Elephants passing the railways station.
Or stay in and play Pot-in-Egg
Or ScrambleJack.
The rocking horse is in the loft.
A yellow fez wearing a monkey
Leads a cow to milk.
Guns are kept in a glass cabinet
Out of reach of their children.
Pop guns, cap guns, Bang! guns,
Stingray Lone Star guns
Green plastic whirring guns

Sparkling space guns.
Weapons of revolution.

The master of the house says:
"You won't dress like Prince William.
I wore a dress until I was eleven
Following the Royals."

Down the stairs
A rolling snake concertina.
Come, we've hardly seen anything.
Some many rooms
You don't have to get back to her anymore.
Play with the robots
Missile robots, radar robots,
Red eyed automatons
Spinning arms, pulsating chest units.
Robot-7. You will be like us.

Magic lanterns
And inappropriate flick-books
Guarded by snapping tin crocodiles
A trophy cabinet of wooden heads
Red cheeked Hitler.
Judy clutches the rag baby
Looks to you for help.
Caress plywood Alice
In this style 10/6.
The white rabbit
(whom you already know intimately)
Shakes a fist
As the Queen of Hearts
Gazes at the sky and wonders.

Teddies in the trees want to play
                    Knucklebones.

Gollies under the table want to play
                Jacks
Space Rangers on the cardboard stages want to play
                Tin whistles
Wax dolls with bandaged fingers
Are washing their hair tonight
And do not wish to play at all.

The Harlequin's curtain is drawn
Over the room at the top of the stairs.
The shadow puppets turn you back
In to the arms of the Matreosehkas
Twelve in all. Rosy red cheeks
Scarf wrapped girlfriends.
Can you name them?

In the alcove,
Other dolls push at the glass
Rock the prams, spill from the toy-chest
Bounce on the sagging mattress
All eyes on you.
Have you brought them a treat?
The wallpaper peels
And the furred monkey rides
The anxious rocking horse
Watches the fences
As a sailor boy casts shells.
We are locked in; how can we harm you?
Welcome Little Man
Squeal the rubber squeaking dolls
Blue bow and she'll show you a promise
True-to-Life face, tight-lipped embarrassment
Happy Tom, the cowboy, is a gossip busy-body.
And the teddy said:
"Asca toooka."

Penny-plain, tuppence coloured
Paper and clay Nagashi-Bina
Float away on the river
Carrying off bad luck.
Ring the pottery bells
When you're done children.

A cellophane birthday treat bag
Tied with red ribbon
Covered in gold stars
Good work.
A blue balloon,
Party popper
Fairy cake and lollypop
A rubber ball and a blue pencil
For all the changes
Happy birthday to you
Happy birthday to you
Happy birthday dear...

Woolner sits in Progress Class
With those who suffer no language
Drown and drawn in acronyms
And gobble up the free toast
Watching for stray bananas
Clap their hands for OFSTED
Tie their hair with postmen's rubber bands
Kick their feet, yell and low five
Kids are crazy you know
They just do what's in their heads.
I still do.
Others ask about the Third World War
Won't talk, won't engage, could do better
Otherwise the colic continues
Clutch the upside down red-eared bunny.
Thin lips stapled shut

They've got a word for that.

Hakeem writes stories of giant crabs.
Out of the sea, cutting off legs.
Leavers sing the same songs again this year.
Husan keeps ladybirds in a jam jar
With jam still in. Don't tell *amma*.
He's got a caterpillar
And two ladybirds
That's all he's got now.
Another bug chewed him up
It kept tickling.
Had one spider
But somebody opened the jar
And it escaped.
He was doing his homework -
For once.
He saw the jar open
And the spider climbed out.
Tried to catch it
But he didn't want to touch it.
Suppose it was a bit big.
He had six ants.
Only that jar didn't have a lid on it.
Out they tumbled
Into the whole house.
Found them in socks,
In sugar, in bed. Don't tell *hoyo*.
His garden is bug garden.
He doesn't take worms indoors
So many worms.
They're not lonely.
He only takes lonely bugs.
Teddy protects me.

So, quite rightly, Shahid says:

We need sixteen minutes
To eat our cake: chocolate & mint,
Served with a scone fork
On Chinese porcelain platters
With a side order of black sticky toffee
But definitely no jam.
Nobody likes grapefruit
But you can have
Gooseberry and cinnamon yoghurt.

Mummi has a big jar
With a picture of Mickey Mouse
On the outside.
I picked it.
Every day we put money in
Coins in, dollars in
Even since we moved here
We spent all the money
On lost property.
My brother spent it all
On fun fair rides.
I won a pink, cute fluffy teddy
Two eyes and a bow.

The kids are getting bored.
So all the children sing:
My lover is an angel, my lover is an angel
My lover is an angel and she goes like this:
Wa, wa, suck my thumb,
Give me a piece of chewing gum
Shush, I'm on the phone
Shh baby's sleeping, shh baby's sleeping,
Do this, do that.
Oh, my aching back!

So all the children sing:

My mummy is a baker
Yum-yummy, fat tummy.
My daddy is a dustbin man,
Poo-poohy, very smelly.
My sister is a show-off
Low skirt, top shelf.
My granddad is a lazy bum
Wrapped his knob in chewing gum.

Charudutta Nadi
Waiting for the bus:
The bus smells too much
Of people who eat medicine
All white beards
And have a stick in their hands
And old clothes
Old people take two seats
They don't go over by the window
They don't look at the water go by
And they have trollies
Sometimes they take off their shoes
Like in a temple
Sticky stink
They eat food and put it in
Their sticky fingers
They eat popcorn and oil
Mix-up. And it makes a smell
And some are just oil
Stink so much
Yesterday on the bus
The oil was burned and smelly,
The door are closed
And it makes big smell.
They don't just smell of cats.
I go on the bus a lot.
My mum, my dad,

Grandma -
She eats medicine -
And my granddad
They eat injections.
They bring their house smell
Put their wheelie-walking chairs
In all the ways
They make a headache
And I am talking to their beards.
They took my toy
Paper – that you make flowers with
And my sister won't share
Old people like flowers
Their fingers struggle to make flowers
Old people
Know how to talk
And then we miss the bus.
And all the toys are sold. Gone.

X

Static in the Green Room
Quick bursts of opera

The church door opens
Mistrust their administrations
The wafer sits awkwardly
Allowed barely a sip of wine.

One elderly Salome, too tired to dance two pews behind
An embarrassed Good Samaritan two pews in front
She whispers her catechisms
And he prays
But still bites into the apple.

Elsewhere Father George
Without a word of a lie
Was preaching to the converted,
Taking great pleasure talking to the elderly
About avoidance of sexual activity and of chastity.
He's not going to change,
No wonder the carol singers
Forgot to turn up come Christmas.
And still he's very difficult to hear
When he's on the altar.

Move on.
Nothing here.
Fact is months ago
I'd tied a wishing luggage label
To Yoko's tree.
That should help.

The banker searches for his wallet
As the beggars dance a tango.

Old Mr Fruish swears under his breath
That it's Tuesday again
But he's not betting certain.

Outside the night truck rocks side to side
As the pigs plot their great escape.

Melanie checks her mobile again
Last chance.
Picks up her bags
And heads off
To the other address.

The workman are all lined up
Across the window chewing hamburgers
Slurping French fries
And worrying about the election.
Naturally, they have their doubts
God help this country.
A lucky dip for tonight?

The manageress
Watches the half-way done man
Take calling cards from the phone box.
Her cigarette tastes stale
Some people have no shame.
Children use washing lines to
Cross from window to window.
The only offer they get
Are the same crisps as yesterday.

xi

This is a pub
What else I am supposed to do?

A large bitter lemon
With a bit a gin in.

That's an old fucking picture
You should see him now
It's an old fucking picture
He's a grey as a chough.
Christ
You asked who it was.
Fuck me. Shoot me down.

Gerry Shapiro
Was a fucking window cleaner,
Subtle as a shit house.

Him and Barry with the cards
Used to drink in the
Pig & Whistle
A short and a stout.
Fucking shock that is.
Don't know who that is
Only a laugh
My boys round here
Was at school with all
Four Barrand brothers.

Don't ask me that
Show me that old picture again.
Ho Chi Minh – no it ain't.
That's definitely
The any old iron man.

He went with
The only fucking woman
I know who can't smile.
Is that Madonna?

So this night
Do you fancy something more
He says
I fancy a curry
He says.
The girl friend at the time
He sent her up the road.
She came back with
Whitebait and cans.
What was she thinking?

Froggy Milligan came out
And took the money
Only stopped for a cup of tea
But we ain't got enough cups.
A cup of tea with a drop of
           Health juice.
I was madder than that.

Alright darlin'
I've been here all day
Pushing me into her tits now, look
I said I'm not being rude
But she's not a princess.
I'm not shagging you on that chair
You need your arse smacking
You're like one of those
Dirty old men.
I am!

Sorry didn't mean to swear.

Old Brillo postie
Comes in with a swag
Full of letters.
He's posting pork
Even when he's drunk.
Ask the nurse
Or the woman from the council
Unless they owe him money
Then he just doing
The fruit machines.

On the bar, by the till,
By the by, a tanner here,
A tanner there. By the wine taps.
Enjoyed a generous glass of Merlot.
Bev's Hospital TV Fund
Pint pot.
Good one. Do one.
Put something on the end of one.
Doctors (& Nurses)
Washed out with soap
And three (or four) in a bed.
Bev has her programmes.
Keep her busy.
Cheers. Be lucky.

Gerald has dyed his hair again
Possum-tailed black comb-over
Look and say what they're not thinking.
Jammed on their seats
Unless they need a top up
No one moves from their circle of friends.
It's not that round. Not my round.

I know that face
I know that fucking face

It's an old picture, so?
Yes it is. Yes, it is.
No, it's not them.
Fuck me; she must be facing back to fifty
She's sticks old.
She showed me some picture from the seventies
Volume 24, issue 2, pages right from centre.
I knew she would be
But I knew she won't.
Brilliant body
But a mouth like
You want to smack it.

Wayne has washed his jacket
Don't get stressed with that
Get on with it, mate.
I had a phone number.
I got Suzi Quatro's
Number if you want it.

Chloe Kay finishes her long drink:
Shooters and Jägerbombs.
Things are desperate.
Desperate as the slashes that
Spiral from wrist to shoulder
On each of her bare arms
Razor scars of continued self-harm
Mirrored in the red runs streaks
That cut through her hair.
As you stand at the bar
She'll tell you her story.
An incoming cold front.

So. Anyway.
Garry Shapiro,
He moved

And married
And I went round one night
I know it's an old photo
But even so
Ten more years in him
If he's got a life.
Don't ever go down
There.
I got the gear on
Fell into bed
A bit in the back like
Thunder her up
Next thing
I'm staying at the station.

He's well famous
Old money
Long time no see
How you been?
Up Scotland.

Laced his coffee,
Laced his tea.
Where's you booze?
All comes out now
She had that dress on for years
Put it in a skip finally.

I know that face.
I know that face.
Rose tattoos
And quick crosswords.
I didn't write to her,
I'm shit at spelling.
It's why I ain't seen
My daughter

For a while.

A glass of wine
In a tall glass
...with ice.
Best be
Of house.

Stagger out
The specials always want to know
Where you're living at the moment.

This one, she's ac/dc.
She comes in with
Her benefit money
Always waits for someone
To turn up.
She says:
All I've done is my hair
What have I done wrong?
What does she mean?
Talking to Julie.
All I was doing
Was talking to Jackie.
She's from the same sing-along.
I had my arm in a sling
She rolled me a fag.

Scaffolding Stew caught the sun.
He's dead now.

This is a pub
What else am I supposed to do?
A tonic water but
Uneasy on the vodka.
I ain't gone.

Show me that picture again.

xii

Open air consultation - one

I am telling you
When my age
Pretend you are young still.
No sitting down.
Behave as if you are going for work.
Don't listen to any relative
Sit down, lay down
Disuse makes atrophy
Life is not for ever
All people go
All the Prophets went.
Any sit down is not good
Quickest way to run down battery
No television that is the secret.
Radio on all the time
Get all news
You won't see me
In front of any television.
With my advice
The cold is only the cold,
The rain is only the rain,
The sun is very good for mood,
Sunshine is in your heart.
Remove your clothes and sit. Only
Not too much. Appreciate it
Only not too much.

Open air consultation - two

The worst disease in the world
Is old age – not cancer.

Cancer has treatment:
Old age none.
Don't waste time
Wishing to be young person
Now their time
Not you.
Be old but keep moving.
I am eighty-plus.
Sun is very good in old age
Keep walking is secret health
Telling people in various countries –
If you don't use sewing machine
It jams
So human body is same.
I have no stick, no help, nothing.
Day and night do good work.
In America they say
Still, sit down person, that is the end.
On the mobile phone
Right to ear
Very bad they say.
Only mobile use in emergency.
No lying down on phone.
You finished.
Also diet
Salt gives hyper-tension
Go out food full of salt and sugar.
The worse place in the world
Is a room old people
Watch all day television.
You finished.
Fat and obese.
Put tomato ketchup everyday –
Is poison.
Once in a while alright.
Not every day.

You live longer with drinking coffee
And coffee prevents bad sleeping.
Better not to have modern things.

Throw TV out of window.
My radio is on twenty-four hours
I get all news of world.

Open air consultation - three

Have a treat but careful
I have one Mr Kipling's Almond slice
The rest health –
You may not look young
But you act young
Getting up
Forcible exercise
Brain exercise
Matching jewellery
Make me think
I am not tired all day.
Little children some tired all day.
People think life is forever
Go on and on
Life is not forever.
People sleep on
Sunday and holiday in bed.
I am always up early.
Joints are not happy
Sitting at home.
Tell everybody:
Getting up,
Washing face,
Putting on make-up
Are all exercise.

Health is a great wealth
You should be poor and healthy.
Do all the good you can,
To as many people as you can,
For as long as you can,
That is the rule I live by.
I have seen many kings and queens
But I am very humble.

Open air consultation - four

You tell your friend
Depression of death
That his wife who left him
All God's will
She's dead
Go to various libraries
Find as many books as he can
Devote time to find books
Read books.
Write down everyday
In diary, on paper
In twenty-four hours
What he did.
How long he thought,
How long he walked,
How long he read.
You will see you are nothing
Don't do nothing.
We cannot say other
But nothing achieved.
Day gone.
Today gone for new baby,
Today gone for old people,
Today gone for all people.

Feel sorry but move always
She dead; you're not.
Okay, it is sadness
You – live. Only chance.
Don't feel sorry
Prophet died,
You will die,
Jesus died,
Everybody die.
God's will.

xiii

A little girl –
Red dress
Spotted with white polka dots –
Holding a purple balloon
Waits for the dinosaur to move.
They will move if you look hard enough,
Look for long enough.
Her brother told her.
Her teacher keeps calling
But she waits.

The ginger-haired kid
Who sat at the front and
Knew all the answers,
Knew all the questions,
Asks:
How are you going to get down?

xiv

Stand on Westminster Bridge
Brown bag of burgers
Throw them in the water?
Or chew them one by one?
Where would they do the most damage?
A life now lived
In meal deals
And cuppa soups
And sandwiches
And toffee crisp McFlurrys.
And packets of Crawford's biscuits –
Digestives and bourbon creams –
And prawn crisps
Taken from the clinic.
There's no taste
To nothing in these.

The mist hasn't rolled back.
The man, unshaven grey,
In frayed jeans
Still wears dark glasses
Watches them in.
Chewing gum cast black
On the paving stones.
Up the stairs an old man
Reads the rugby
Barely glances
All he needs to know.
October cold and fully attended.
Coffee? instant. Tea?
Handful of Smarties?
White cups, no saucers.
Laid out like a Travelodge room
Just a Scarlett Johansson poster

On the opposite wall
And the biscuits are
McVitie's plain chocolate digestives.
"What do you want to talk about?"
I don't care.
"Just talk about Scarlett."
I could pretend I didn't listen
... but I'd be lying. Again.

Occasionally someone will stop,
Thought I recognised that beard.
She's married well
And didn't tell anyone.
I'm very well.
I thought it was you.
And the dwarf
Asks if we know
What he means.

Aunty Peggy and Carole
Have a tête-à-tête
Whilst I'm not there,
Sister.
So many difficulties.
He had two Oyster cards,
Never know the one to take.
Have to get the fiver back.
Just want someone
To ask:
"Do you need anything?"
Obviously at home
She'll have a cup of coffee,
He'll have a tea.
Four or five?
Not four or five, maybe three.
That's different from last time.

Illness creates differences,
Mainly unforeseen,
Maybe structural.
As I said:
I've got his keys.
Be miserable at home,
Worrying about mum
She's not going to go away.
Ultimately, it's about home,
Aunty Peggy and my sister
Moving funerals forward.
Everyone is tidy if they can make it,
All rushing, rushing when they get there.
A weekend would make a lot of time.
Palmer Lawful told about time.
Unless he has come back.
Can't hang about too long
Depends what the doctor finds.
Hallelujah.
Couldn't be arsed to shave.
Passers-by in wide hats
Are a little scared.
Ideally the whole place should be cleared out
Aired out –
      but there's nobody there
                    - to air it out.

After every death
Who asks why?

The church bells were ringing
All the morning
Could be to do with
The Battle of Britain.
The sound of a Spitfire –
Nothing like it
Grandma had a Spitfire badge

Made from an actual Spitfire
Got lost in the going away
When she was called up.
Put the news on
Didn't see it all.

The ants were there again,
Those ants that took the third hat
As the taxi was delayed.
These ants got into Melissa's knickers
At the Battersea Travelodge
Where she worked as a night manageress,
Chambermaid and bottle-washer porter.
A guy vomited on her blouse.
Something was wrong
With the pink champagne.
The girls were all laughing.
Can you have me now?
I've never done anything like this before
So please be kind.
Hear it again, her first time.
I'm not going to spoil
Inside you – promise.
Yet the next morning
The morning after pill
Costs over twenty quid.
Still turns up for work
Which explains why she's single.
Perhaps.
And...
Anyway that's what people say.

XV

I like that one, daddy.
Another one. No, this one.
Look at that one. And red.
Music to go with it?
Daddy, I want to get down now.
There's a woman, can you see her?
That's exactly who she is.
Daddy, what's that? There's one there.
I like that one: all rainybowed.
Daddy, why do I see peacocks?
Shall we dance, daddy?
Look at the colours over there.
Dance! Dance! Dance! Daddy, dance!
Wailing – dance! Crying – dance.
                          Dance – please.
Daddy, you're here.

You are here.
In the underpass,
Shapes huddled in sleeping bags.
A melt room
Of ideas and
Blunt opinions.
In the alleyway
Beside the Oxford Street works
Drilling and hammering,
Broken eggshells
And fried chicken skins.
Constant drizzle.
Tucked into a corner
Blue sleeping bag, canvas holdall pillow
Clutching a chewed Styrofoam cup
Containing 11p in coppers.
An opened pack of macaroons
And a Tesco sausage:
Freshly baked instore.
Card sign:
Very hungry
I am so desperate
For a night off the streets
Please have a ♥
Share a cigarette with
The peacock girl,
Her left arm covered with tattoo feathers
The neck and beak pecking at her throat.
Pretend it's you birthday
Share the soup – pink or white.
Arm in arm
Good window shopping
If I could buy you the world
A mannequin opens a yellow umbrella

Create your own sunshine.
Walk along the road
Where I first worked
Everything has changed.
Even the betting shop has vanished.

"Hello, can you let me in?"
He's still there pressing the buzzer.

Even on the Friday
Fancied baked beans one day,
Got the tin out
Couldn't believe it.
Got bloody pickled sausage in it.
Well I have got the sausage
Hid the baked beans
Picked it out for me
Tinned sausage: oh, how revolting,
Sausage in tins,
Sausage in tins!
It must be disgusting, mustn't it?
Party-fancy sausage
As a normal rule I don't eat beans
Especially baked.
For a change I though
Two tins in the cupboard, each
With one sausage.
I wouldn't have bought it
You wouldn't have bought it
Who would have bought it?
That Stan would have bought it
He never looks at a label
Ignores the picture for the lettering.
Useful rule of thumb
Never eat sausage from a can.
I wonder if it's a skinned one. Still

You couldn't even dress it up
To look kosher.

The Chinese woman
In the leopard skin
Gets a ticket.
She needs to change her name.
Shouts at the traffic warden
Who right now only speaks Swahili.

Anna-Maria grimaces
As skin touches skin.
Skin gets thinner, bleeds easier.
Nineteen ragbags head to Africa.

Karla and Orlanda,
Round and round
Sloane Square,
Bright red baby,
Brighter red romper,
German lullabies.
Always best to be born abroad.

Diamonds and banks:
    "I did it all so quickly."
Puppets and personal fragrances:
    "I got a bit lost."
Outside the Hotel:
    "You must keep your jacket on, sir."
Wedding dresses and grass skirts
Crowds push your face up to the glass.

Gerry came back from south east Asia
With a brand new Cambodian bride -
Soportevy, a blind masseuse.
All above board.

She likes England,
Fitted right in.
She had a feel for it.
Comes up to their silk and fine linen
Wedding anniversary come May.
Who'd have thought?

The namer of clouds died here.
Do you want to talk about it?

On the bad end of a Cricklewood kebab,
The Fermanagh man
Uses last Thursday's Evening Standard
To wipe the blood from his nose
And ask:
Can you help me out?

I'll come and see you occasionally
You might recognise the dress
        it was blue before.
Red wine through a straw.
That's a Babushka scream
You'll hear them more often
Like cutlery raking across fine porcelain.
On the outskirts of Heaven
All the doors are white.
There are so many doors
In His house.
So many rooms.
A phrase heard too often
In recent years.

In front the weather-worn
Still watering eyes of Samuel Beckett,
The waiting artist must
Remember to smile

At strange men
Who, standing about
For an hour and a half,
Query: are you trying to make me?
Place ready ripe sunflowers in her lap
And thank her for listening.
So say: goodbye. Not working.
A last glass of early morning red.
Record a life on scrapes of paper,
Pocket full of notes.

The night porter slips out
To write to his friend.
"Yeah, you're alright, Wes
We knock it all down
Then we build it all up again
Exactly the same."

xvii

Walk along the wall
Keep your balance.
The camera will record each pose.
Take off the cheesecloth dress.
Only instead of white lingerie,
She is naked.
I move to hastily cover her.
"I thought that's what you wanted."
It is.
Of course it is
But not in front of all these people.
I don't know what I'm saying,
I wait for months
And then rush to wake up.

People like you.

People like her.

And the others?
Past girlfriends.
Recall odd events.
One wants to be important
It's coming to something, isn't it?
Head down to Brighton,
Sit on the beach and play about
Got more and more spiteful.
We'll meet up at the Harvester,
Could call it a date
Thursday
Not too wonderful
Expecting a lot.
Can you remember their names?
Make a list.

Upstairs what needs cleaning?
Look at you now.
"How many Page 3 girls did you
Sleep with in the late seventies,
Early eighties?"
Can you remember their names?
Surely you remember their names.

Close your eyes.
Whose face do you see?
Is that any surprise?

People like you
Need people like me.

People like her.

How does the argument go?
Lie down,
She can feel your ribs.
The flat now feels cold
Unlived in apart from
Hours like this.

How can you not touch?

Wish we were saying instead.

The horse hospital – closing down,
A doorway next door.
No sign.
I got the letter from you
Unsealed,
Unwritten.
By the time we'd got there –
    We'd never met.
All four of us,
Well most of us,
Don't hang around the right place.
Never been there without you.
Had a standing invitation since the word go.

Kick the empty bottle
Rolls across the smooth wood
But the ballet dancers/
Belly dancers are long gone.
The Tai Chi members
Watch
Leave a hand print on their mirror.

Pretends she can hear the rattling of loose change

Buy me just another day, another hour.
I can lend you a pound
Frequently folded.

Jazzman advises:
Take your seat please
Everything is about to kick off.
Names are called on Sunday,
A constant karaoke.
Tim'll sing a song of dark roads
And thin, thin lines
Walked any time,
Like he really means it.
Because he does.
Absolutely.
If in doubt please just read the lyrics.
James'll translate in to Korean
Or now, more likely, Mandarin.
And Helen'll be there, of course,
To explain what's going on.
Tough act to follow.
There's not enough window to open.

Then my wife said:
How long can you..?
The rest is interrupted
By the Third Samaritan
In the airless room
And a ringing telephone.

There's a bit of history
Just thought I'd mention it.
Two steps forward,
Three back
And one to the side.

And, as calm as custard,
She says:
I just thought I'd let you know
I'm pregnant.

People like you
Have people like her.

People like you.

People like her.

xix

I am a sinner
Do you know him this evening?
All flesh is grass
God wants to speak to some of you
Here one minute, gone the next
We are the Church of the Street
Knock and the door will be opened.

Get yourself ready to meet Jesus
Or you go to Hell fire
Only two places
Hell is a dangerous place, my dearest friends
Make up your mind today
Jesus loves you.
You know the problems.
You cannot help yourself.
Only Jesus will.
If you are sick
Go to the hospital or the GP
Even if they come to your house
Unless you come to Jesus
There is no cure
Jesus will solve your problem
To the world's sick problems
He knows what sucks at your mind.

Dancing in circles
Shouting for Jesus
Share your testimonies
Here to tell you God loves you
Sunday School Jesus loves you
Died for you.
Experience that love
Forgiveness – right now

Hope restarted – right now
Assurances when you die – right now
Look at the newspaper
Something isn't right.
You fell short

Sleeping outside of marriage: I've done that
Stealing time: I've done that
Lying: I've done that
How many messages can you listen to?

I am talking to you,
Don't turn you back.

We are the Church of the Street
And you have been chosen.
We are the Church of the Street
And you have been singled out.
We are the Church of the Street
God knows you've suffered loss.

XX

wear carpet slippers
sweep the stage
these are prime seats
keep the ticket
as a souvenir

I made a reservation for the play.
Thought it might be a juvenile drama.
It's a proper play
With proper words
And everything.
It's bloody expensive.
Can't we give all this up?

Enjoy the show.

Cut out and colour,
Paste the backdrop,
Some kind of pantomime,
Cinderella maybe
Or Treasure Island
Probably the Snow Queen.
Open the shadow box.
Careful now,
She'll break easily.

One of those days, these days
Still got my flat
Catch up, meet up.
Why move from an area you know?
Driving through the town
A deer ran out
Just going for afternoon tea
One of those things.

113

The brunette rolls naked on the carpet
"You've lost weight," she says
As the boats drift by.
The moorings are deserted.
Coffee.
Digestive biscuits.
She talks constantly:
I like lemon drizzle cake
Chocolate berries and cream.
You're in charge of the candles
Do you put candles on black forest gateaux?
I must have candles
Let's make a fairy cake.
A school friend who had a baby or...
Went to prison really early
When I worked in Derry.
Well, I'd go to Tesco for flat tin cake
She worked in Tesco
Must have cake not cheese biscuits.

The Husband:	Try my key.
	Things are much better
	when I am not here.
The Wife:	When did it start raining?
The Husband:	Nine o'clock.
The Wife:	Nine?
The Husband:	Nine o'clock.
The Wife:	It hasn't rained for a long time.
The Husband:	It washes the streets
The Wife:	Badly needs it.
The Husband:	Still no sign.
The Wife:	Well Ann usually gets her hair done
	on a Friday.
The Husband:	Her man; is he working?
The Wife:	He's working.

The Husband:	Is it a paying job?
The Wife:	Charity.
	He works up the charity shop.
	It's not cold today.
The Husband:	No, it's very warm, very close.
	Do you want a sweet?
The Wife:	I had one not long ago.
The Husband:	Let the tea cool down.
	Shall I fetch your walking stick?
The Wife:	Where's Ann? Tell her bad news
The Husband:	And she smiles.
The Wife:	Gets her hair cut
	and the colour put in it Fridays.
The Husband:	A lot of people downstairs.
	Standing around the table
	drinking. What a thing to do.
The Wife:	Her sister never gave her the note.
The Husband:	That's why we never heard from them.
The Wife:	She never goes out.
The Husband:	She's crippled.
The Wife:	The note was for Thomas.
	Needed to get a bigger size.
The Husband:	What size is this?
The Wife:	Pull it up. Marie will know.
The Husband:	Always trust braces.
The Wife:	And a white shirt.
The Husband:	Do you want to get ready?
The Wife:	I don't mind. We can do.
	Take the old flowers,
	wrap them in orange plastic.
	Where's David?
The Husband:	If it clears up,
	he'll be in the park.
The Wife:	He likes to be doing someone.
The Husband:	It's good for him as well.
The Wife:	No word from Joseph?

The Husband:	He has to let the builders in.
The Wife:	He's paid for that?
The Husband:	Oh, yes.
	Get a week now,
	a week later.
The Wife:	Have a rest after lunch.
The Husband:	Told me to remind you.
The Wife:	Will there be a cup of tea
	if I stay here?
The Husband:	The family will come.
The Wife:	Even Natalie off the corner?
The Husband:	Blessed for all that.
The Wife:	And her with a Methodist mother too.
The Husband:	Can't choose family.
The Wife:	Is Ted Cottle out the hospital?
The Husband:	Ted Cottle?
The Wife:	Yes, Ted Cottle.
The Husband:	He's doing fine.
The Wife:	Is he? And his wife?
The Husband:	She never goes out
	She's crippled see.
The Wife:	So think the finish to that then.

The boxer crouches in the corner
Tyre treads for gloves:
Bound and torn
White rivets run
Red-nosed neighbour
Glancing over the fence
Mr & Mrs Chappell-Gardener
Check the papers are burnt well.
Miss Pershouse sits on the only green chair,
Paper rose in her hair,
Selling raffle tickets.
Prizes included:
Sticky toffee pudding (barely touched)

And a ten-year old blue budgerigar.
The jigsaw remains of party ring biscuits
Lie at her bare feet.
No more services washes
Rain windows
Pale Jess' blushes, pink
As a plate of prawns
Is set on the table.
A man of few words
Holds the blue string.
Crab claws: will that do?

(That's where we should have come in
You mean?)
(Not necessarily).
(So what's going on, James?)

Shaun in a green onesie
Passes the empty gasometer
Ms Tugpenny sits in the garden
Hoping for avocets.
Mr Johnson's cataracts are deeper.
Today's news is vague.
My wife at the sink? Yellow hair?
Green? Brown? Tan? Dress
Washing her hair? Washing the potatoes?
Check pockets for loose change.
How much do I need today?
Tuppence for a smile.
Penny for a song.
Tanner for a squeeze.
A shilling all gone.
Hard-boiled egg. Wholemeal soldiers.

Take the next book from the shelf
Paint black flowers on

Pages 275 through to 297,
Whistle about sunlight,
Draw dancers on
Pages 426 up to 469.
Keep it simple you're saying?

Look at it closely
At distance the idea is clear.
His wife is on every page.
A hand print.

The man in the wheelchair
Won't give up.
Would you save a dandelion
In a glass?
The man next door,
With the noted liver spots, weeps.
He wanted white wine instead.

How do you know all that?

Sensible Sharon dresses men
Insists on white Y-fronts
That do little for him – just my opinion.
Have you still got that bloody green jumper?
How old was he then?
Brush the origami animals aside
Zebra, crabs, kingfishers.
Always elephants.
It is strictly forbidden to touch.

Are you going to miss France this year?
(Ce ne doit pas être rendue publique).
Her shitty sisters argue
Over fish, the dog's eyes
As it pisses by the table,

Pisses by the door,
Pisses on the carpet,
Won't invite no more.

A shopping trolley full of pig heads
Rolls downhill. Trots over the cobbles.
Dried poppy heads rattling.
But she's famous
Bead box. Treasure trove.
Buy an empty box
(What do you do with inappropriate between-spaces?)

People don't realise how dangerous the water is
Quickmud. I'll tell you what there is
Up to your waist. Porous clay.
Came out though different colours.
Really pretty. All kinds of things like that
On the foreshore. Go mud picking.

(Are you well known?)
No, but I like the old Sunday school teacher
Who pushes the wheelchair.

Phyllida sits patiently with her sister
Going to the park too
Nice to get out at our age
Speak to the chef. Speak to the parson.
Speak to the puppeteer.
Tasteless shepherd's pie
Upmarket super market.
Drown in Worcester Sauce.
Don't forget:
Keep it down, fellas.

Jessy and Lauren drop poppies
And can't look each other in the face

Clementine gets it
Sassy and appetent
Why are you all hanging back?
To be polite.

It looks like ... an unpleasantness?
(Ich muss weg von London zu bekommen).
That's what the taxi driver needs to know.

Every aspect yells sensible.
Alabaster skin. Dark black shoes.
Blue jumper (dark). Art scarf (darkish)
Black skirt. (Can't buy darker).
Shoulder length brown hair (on the dark side).
Checks her book.
She has something so precious
You wouldn't sell it, would you?
She won't meet you in a restaurant
Because of your advancing years
Yet her eyes tell you
She knows where the car is parked.

That's pretty.
Can you see a horse?
(Goodness knows what that's supposed to be).
Don't spend too long in this room.
The sheep just felt like a conversation.

Can't really go on
Part people
People part.
People part
All the time.
Staying together is the trick.

Leave some of the words out

Put this at the end on purpose
I see love and I have to walk on.

(Don't understand a word
But it was very well done).

xxi

Same street.
You know these streets well.
"Do you understand where we're heading yet?"

The lawyer chases a tumbling umbrella
And paper aeroplanes
Across the park.
Mr & Mrs Banerjee throw sticks.
"We're locking up for the night.
It's late. You can't stay here."

"You've spent a long time away."
Broken branches litter the path.

"Got any spare principles, mate?"

Sitting on the bench
At the edge of the garden
Someone else turns.
I seem to remember the name.
"I am going to let you down."
"How do you know that?"
"Is it alright if I say no?"
"Why would you say no?"
"I might. Might not."
"Is it alright if I keep asking though?"
"Still friends?"

Walk past the benches
Read the inscriptions
Familiar names.
My wife and love of my life,
Lunch and moments shared
Breakfast, a walk, a bench

Ever & always
This beautiful square holds her secrets
Who loved to walk
Almost as much as her husband loves her
Home is wherever we can gather together
Who found her love in London
In our dream, in our life,
Never another you
Felt the magic and found joy
Celebrate your calm beauty.

Can't hear the nightingale
For the constant traffic.

The sandwich-board men
Stand opposite
Arrows pointing
Signs waving.

Remember now.
Back in the day at rush-hour
Oxford Circus
Man in a raincoat,
Flat cap.
Stanley Green.
LESS LUST
BY LESS
PROTEIN:
MEAT, FISH
BIRD; EGG
CHEESE
PEAS BEANS:
NUTS
AND SITTING.
Acknowledging God
In case there happens to be one.
Eight Passion Proteins.
DONATION 7P
BOOKLET FREE.

A police car blocks the
Burger King
Drive-through.

A corral of burnt out cars
Partially submerged.
Barrett carries a bag of hamburgers
To dole out to

The self-made squatters,
To share with rum and rancour.

Outside the multi-storey
Minnie Mouse asks me if
I'd like a fresh Argos catalogue
There, bored, if I'd break Rule 34.
The felt-tip black dot on the end of her nose
Twitches enticingly.

Through Brick Lane.
Mayley & Godwick
Playing drums
In the amp-up back of a white Ford Transit
Passing the audition.
The curry touts stand uneasy
In the restaurant doorways
Discussing aspects
Of salty water and change.
Aloo chop 50p
Prawn puri & to follow lamb green masala,
Spinach or onion pakora
Yet Piglet and Eeyore have been starved
And tied to a drain pipe.

Keri Kutz – trading as normal
The sign curled and tanned
Window sellotape stained
Half a dozen monochrome hair styles
Portraits from the 50s and 60s
Sophia Loren rest on the sill
Black framed, attracting dust
Bills Stickers will be prosecuted
Hidden by fliers for
Don't Boo Me Off The Stage 2,
Every Weekend House

Circus Fantasia up the Common
Wrestling:
Thirty man over the top rumble
Tough Times Handicap Match
Tiger Tom Turner up against
The Brixton Brickhouse
In the Long Way Home Tag Team Challenge
Last dance Lockdown
One Time Moses
Face to face with
Ding Dong Harris.
Bell time 7 p.m.
In the shop
The Hair sign
Rolled up daffodil carpet
White front doors
A mattress for overnights
Ironing boards.
All the painted is chipped
Pizza leaflets jut from
The peeling enamel letter box.

Alam rattles his coffee can
On the corner of
Charlotte Street.
Holds a white board
For the business women

EAM MUTE
HAVEND
DIABETIS, MONI
FOR MEDICINE
FOR FOD PLIS
GOD BLESS YOU
TANKYU YOU
ALAM

He reads lips.
We talk of home,
Of old friends,
Of novels and
A string of words.
In the buttonhole
Of his mouse grey jacket
He wears a yellow gerbera
Taken from the Newman Street Tavern.
Ignored on the empty glass table,
The bloom suits him more.

And my wife says:
How long can you hold..?
In the distance
Faint sirens begin
Draw in closer
Almost time then.

Tambourines and finger cymbals
Hear the clatter of the Krishnas
But it fades rapidly away.
Homeless.
"Hungry mate, hungry."
Three coats – a cold, bitter day.
The Witness, Awake, outside Ladbrokes
Offers two copies of each magazine.

Gary's in trouble
Smoked every single one
No word of a lie.
Paddy wants some snuggie
But there's none to be had
And a loud voice for shrile
Will get you nicked like that.

"I wouldn't do that to you.
Never," he tells Moroccan.
Solomon hands out the remedies,
Klarybel or Sibilia ask if I'm looking for succour:
The last knocking of old Soho as we pass.
Not here. Not today.

Todd drags his one-wheel case
On by into the Co-op
And from behind the till Bharti stares.
She is hoping for a better day
Without broken mirrors
But there's nothing anybody can say.
Halfway between nowhere,
All he wants is mouthwash.
The case is jammed full
Of American Astronaut comic-books,
Google-eyed Robert Crumb,
Freak Brother's omnibus, original Maus
Fat Freddie's Cat, one copy of Moomin.
He asks four times but only gets a grin.
Throws a bunch of yesterday's yellow roses
Across from the window to the bakery section.
"Bastards blanking me cos I ain't from round here."
A shower of curled petals float on to the donuts,
Settle on the brown multi-seed triangular rolls.
"Please God."

The Cut Girl
Hasn't come out
To skip or chase again today.
And the lace curtains are still
Hanging heavy in the white windows
Although the scaffoldings remains up.
The wood has rotted through.
Nobody's been on the roof

To cut the grass or trim the bush.
No one's pulled at the purple flowers.
Beth diligently cuts the string,
Dave opens the last of the wine,
Shannon makes paper-toys.

Tea and cake was all I had
And you want a fight.
Tea and cake is all I ever have.
So the DJ asks:
"What's happening Dagenham tonight?"
"It's calm," says Kerry. "Give it a go."
Push the guttered, shattered watermelon aside.
Wipe the seeds from your shoes.
Harry H. hauls the fruit & veg wagon homeward.
The green and white striped tarpaulin
Prayer mat is rolled away
Outside the pop up Mosque.
The market's closed: can't you read?

Catalina Manchola sells the Issue,
Flowers shining in his bobbed hair.
Wide glasses and full red lips –
"We are all someone
From somewhere different."
In an accent that's hard to place:
"You want change? God bless."

Under the red Chinese lanterns
Women in pink puffa jackets
Stand outside restaurants constantly waving
Without making eye contact
Like so many Lucky Cats
In the deserted 10p shovel
Pusher penny falls.
No one's playing the game.

Orange chickens and ducks sweat.
Poles argue outside the betting shop.
Bubble tea and dim sum lie in wait.
Boxes of fortune cookies on special
Forever breaking until the right message
Crumbs ignored by the pigeons
Paper dragons coil through
Patchouli and jasmine scented incense.
"Hello, massage?" changes nothing.
We've got to that point
Where she knows.
A hundred waving cats.
Are they all so lucky?

The door is open this afternoon
Hand-scribbled enticements
1st floor
Nicky: no rush
Good services.
Private parties
And groups
Catered for.
Top floor. Tall leggy New Laura
Dark stairs. No carpet.
Hear you coming
Single red 60w bulb.

Into Old Compton Street,
Which goes nowhere much:
Just here and there,
The bouncers stand guard
Outside Ann Summers
Turning ha'penny customers away.
Or are they simply window shopping?
Or waiting for the Duke of Wellington to run dry?
Or have they wandered

From next door's premise with tables
Or simply further down Las Vegas pool hall?

Presley, Elvis badges weighing him down,
Crosses without looking.
From a hastily arranged soap-box,
A trio of sweet transvestites condemn austerity.
Michael Jackson's coat proves
All that glitters is not gold.
Claire dries her eyes,
Takes a deep breath
At the stage door
But something doesn't feel right.

At the corner of the Square
The Grim Reaper poses
Before the Gallery
Photos for tourists
His plastic scythe above their heads
As he dances to the steel drums.
Jugglers warm up
As fools rush in
Close by witches, golden goblins and Yoda
In an 'I love London' t-shirt
Cheap robes caught in the wind.
Moved on by the Heritage Wardens.

Children leap for giant bubbles
That drift, sparkle and flex
Caught in the briefest light.
The curled serpent bites the coin
That feeds him
As MOMOX rubs chalk dust from his fingertips.
School girls draw hearts
On the grey pavement.
Karla y Andreas forever.

I miss my wife
Even more when the sun shines.
Skateboarders don't see the steps.
Luther picks change from the grass
Pleased to see ya, my man.
Also good to see
Roxanne has still got her purple party hat on.

Bemoaning the decline of magic,
The wizard has long since
Rolled up his star cape,
Stuffed his broom in a polka dot shopping trolley
And returned to his bedsit in Clerkenwell.

Under an arch, filled up with two,
A busker sings Sweet Caroline
The chorus drowned by traffic.

A rabble of school children
Waved away across the wide road
Although the man is red
Matching their jumpers.

The Horse guard watches
The men hose away any evidence
Clean streets round here.
As camera phones whine and click
The horse remains calm
As does the armed police officer.
Police helmets – two pounds.

An elderly man, left unattended,
Hands me D-Day: a guide for eternal salvation.

Thirty more children in maroon
Look at that

More police, a bit too early,
Watch the plebs shuffle and tumble
Follow a trail
Of crumples scratch cards.
Talk about the gypsies out for a day.

Stop. Do not proceed
Beyond this point
Until instructed by the guard.

Mile after mile of crush barriers.
Keep out? Keeping in?
Protestors throw traffic cones
Police batons raised
For democracy. Withdraw.
I have done nothing wrong.
Green smoke. Back off.
Drag the woman by her hair.

Plump woman in a rose blouse
Smokes another cigarette
Red telephone boxes filled with lost tourists
Looking for college student, school girl Alex, Italian stunner.

The artist, once a doctor, sits in front of Churchill
Cloth cap, raincoat for the weather
Paints the Palace in subtle watercolours
Arches, turrets, clock face, once again.
A union flag flapping from his easel
Directions and donations
Where's Big Ben?
Painting keeps him out of mischief:
Is that what you want?
Take this to remember me –
A sketch of St Paul's.
I do remember the scene:

Standing on the rain swept portico
Behind the Corinthian columns
And unopened oak West Doors.
Just a changed man under a spell
Waits putting together the pieces
Across a slippery chequer board.
A Singapore bride, hair tied,
Her bare shoulders tanned and dripping
Dress draped over the steps.
A bridegroom, in sodden black jacket,
Holds her hand and smiles.
Like a vision she brushes rain from his collar
As the camera fires.
What does the downpour matter?
Wipes the drips from her eyelashes
Pose for the wide shot.
Suddenly they are being shooed off
By an unforgiving official
Who confused happiness for lost revenue.
This church is a house of trade.
No joy even on the steps.
What would Jesus do?
That placard long gone
Pulled away by bailiffs
As Occupy London
Stood for the 99%
And the money changers
Grazed their knees
And cursed into their
Frothy cappuccinos.
Queen Victoria in a
We are the Anonymous mask.
Don't take pictures,
Take action.
I waited for a friend
Who won't recognise me today.

Each artist continues
Now you should ask:
Where's The Peace Man?
Dear Brian, ten years outside
Dead and gone, I tell them.
Ought to be a statue.
A Blue plaque at least.

A Japanese woman
Takes a swig from the bottle
Disguised in a Tesco bag.

Across the square the bell tolls four.
Except no one listens.

Pass holders only at St Stephen's.
Victoria Tower Gardens are deserted.
The news has moved on,
The camera crews all abroad now.
Rake women hand in hand.
Where do you want to go?
Do you know the code?
You don't look like you belong.

Two Caribbean nurses push a stretcher
The patient's face closed, eyes closed, oblivious
Although she is quite enjoying the sun.
Slowly, slowly, she wants to be recognised.
She has a message – nice weather for it.

The smell of piss and shit and statistics
Washed off in warm water and pink soap
Masked by the scent of sandalwood and jasmine.

In the underpass the Romanian accordionist

Plays a local song that echoes off the tiles.
Polish women offer fish & chips.
The Sikh in the blue turban
Rubs his pepper beard thoughtfully
As the pigeons gather underfoot hoping for blood.
Duma, the professional street performer,
Jumps through hoops from a height.
Horses eternally circle chased by a dragon
Morris dancers and skate boarders fight
About what tonight they forget.
The legendary wizard licks a super soft.
An impatient crowd gathers,
Calling for him to turn on the lights,
Hoping to hear him say:
Here is my dragon: Temba Chesin,
Blue scaled and short-horned (only..,
You're not supposed to know that).
As Happy Larry walk away with arms full
Of books and pamphlets
That'll never be missed especially the poetry and plays.

Outside Sainsbury Local
The woman from the bridge
All those days, weeks, months ago,
The woman in the worn wheelchair
We pushed homeward one afternoon.
On this saturated November afternoon –
A straw sunhat to keep off the rain
Constant as the hem of Abigail's skirt
Crosses London. Taking its time.
Waves me over:
Could you buy me a steak pie?
75p they are.
Anything else?
Some baby leaf spinach?
I add some custard creams.

Thank you, darling.
Her hand is frozen,
Skin worn tight.
I forget her name.
Lili. For Lili Marlene
Named after my aunt's great grandmother
She kept the troops happy
Not like nowadays
Wars all over
And us expecting bombs here.
Awful.
Lili Marlene.
That's not bullshit. That's true.
What's your name?
I tell her.
Timothy Whites? She jokes.
They eventually disappeared.
Went the way of Woolworths.
How long had she been waiting here?
How long left this time?

Electricity workers lean on the barrier
Stare at the hole, stare at the pipes. S.E.P.
Someone Else's Problem.
I understand you
I understand mum
But she's gone for a day
To Southend but not to touch the sea
Or watch an amateur dream play.
Nothing to worry about
Although you're an animal
Seriously
Johnson sits on the edge of the hole.
Cut the blue or the green?
Reg puts his fingers in his ears.

The cabby will take you
Wherever you want to go.
No questions asked.
A tall man with a malicious grin
Pulls a catalogue from a Top Shop bag
And asks me
If I want to fuck something.
He speed-dials and everyone,
All the Bright Young Things,
The trained, eager boys and girls,
Answer their mobiles instantly.

Dark
And a shaven-headed woman
Asks me the way.
Do I like choice?
Strides away
Without a reply
Clutching a green paperback:
An Afterlife of Memories.

Against her better judgement,
Jennifer Crossland
Has come into town
Booked a Travelodge room,
Knows what you're here for.
The years since
Weren't roses and chocolate.
How many times did you put the phone back down?
On the corner
Kids play fipple flutes
As the neighbour's husband
Treats his wife, a Bank Holiday princess,
Splashing out at Wetherspoons.
Hold a posy of St Brigid anemones,
Always an eye for colour.

What are you staring at now?
No school today, dress up.

London Fields
Shutters down, deserted concrete
And No Parking and a now-cold pie.
Deep in the heart of Hackney.
Loneliness gets into your bones,
Face off the corner boys,
Pavements gritty underfoot.
Up the yellow staircase,
Echoes and crimson-copper cockroaches.
The centre-bound platform almost deserted.
Only one briefly silent man
Waiting for the slow train.
Tear at the newspapers
Cracked earth and acid-stained glass
That's your reflection in the wrong mirror,
The same people in different rooms.
Sit down. Is this one spare?
Einstein sat there once upon a time.
A glass of red
Will be finished in time for the last bus.
I blame the Mayor
Lies and smears and distortions.
The man says:
People stop me in the street
- we're overcrowded, they moan.
Violent attacks on people who look different.
The old day's union rep never silent,
Always with a left-field book open,
On his two half-hour tea-breaks.
If you don't like nasty people
Cross the road more often.
Sitting in a Turkish restaurant with Boris.
Boris is no fool.

And the funny things is...
Who is running this show now?
The reporter from the Morning Star
Whispers conspiracies in her editor's ear.
Looking at doors, looking at window cards
For a room to afford.
Teachers need to just come in and teach.
The train shudders around the bend.
- Thank you for listening.
The man, obviously older since our last meeting,
Autographs the expanse

London belongs to all of us.

Ken

Here we have pictures of the scene.
They really set the scene
If you've seen this scene.
Along the Thames wall four clay figures,
Terracotta and stoneware,
Sitting knees drawn up.
Lying on their sides, knees to chest,
Protecting against a twist of fate,
Asleep on the black marble.
Drawing a crowd.

Southwark Bridge
Down the side stairs
To the green spiked metal gate
Always padlocked tight.
So bright boy, you asked earlier,
How am I going to get down?
I will tell you now -
Wayne Wilson half-inched the padlock,
Stole it on a BOGOF

(Burgle one, get one free). Special deal.
Plus a seventeen peak Toblerone,
Lifted from Budgens.
Don't ask where he stashed it.
A gift for my mother:
Happy Easter.
   Happy Christmas.
     Happy Birthday.

Happy?

My mother –
Now that's someone
We haven't spoken about.
How will she view all this
Nonsense?
I told you so?
No, my mother possesses more subtlety
But that's another story
That now will not be told.

Having said that –

Listen….
That metallic tearing?
The opening of a fresh can of worms.
Family-sized. 20% extra free.

The gate swings open.
Even though I know what happens next
I treat the algae and mud-coated steps down
With the due care and attention.
Still hearing sirens.

<u>xxiii</u>

Bollocks
Bloody hell
The water's cold!

I think about that quite a lot.

My wife says to me:
How long can you hold your breath?

I think about that quite a lot too.

Then,
Wiltshire echoing in each word,
She says:
Please, my love,
Let me take you home.